Lonely Planet

POCKET

TENERIFE

TOP SIGHTS · LOCAL EXPERIENCES

P9-DHG-913

LUCY CORNE, DAMIAN HARPER

Contents

Plan Your Trip 5

Anaga Mountains (p140)
BAIGOZIN/SHUTTERSTOCK ©

Welcome to Tenerife

Tenerife is the striking grande dame in the Canaries archipelago. Attracting over six million visitors a year, the island's famous southern resorts offer Brit-infused revelry combined with sandy beaches and all-inclusive resorts. But get your explorer's hat on and step beyond the tourist spots and you'll discover an island of extraordinary beauty and diversity, with remote mountain-ridge villages, cultured port settlements and charming old towns.

Auditorio de Tenerife (p46), designed by Santiago Calatrava, Santa Cruz de Tenerife

Top Experiences

Museo de la Naturaleza y el Hombre

Hospital converted into a tantalising museum. **p38**

Mercado de Nuestra Señora de África

Santa Cruz' definitive, delightful market. **p40**

Tenerife Espacio de las Artes (TEA)

Outstanding architecture and art space. **p36**

Parque Nacional del Teide
Spain's highest point. **p134**

Casa de los Balcones
Heritage icon of La Orotava. **p96**

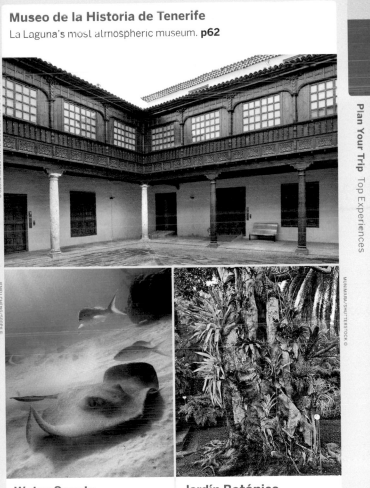

Museo de la Historia de Tenerife

La Laguna's most atmospheric museum. **p62**

Water Sports

Into the big blue. **p24**

Jardín Botánico

Tenerife's outstanding botanical wonderland **p78**

Eating

Tenerife's cuisine has moved on dramatically from its humble beginnings and today the island's restaurant scene is home to five restaurants with six Michelin stars between them. These days tourists can ditch the buffet in favour of more appealing and imaginative dishes, ranging from traditional Canarian cuisine, typified by robust homestyle cooking, right through to the tantalising haute cuisine of gastro temples, where innovative chefs serve some fabulously novel fusion combinations.

IMV/GETTY IMAGES ©

Island Specialities

Canarian cuisine reflects Latin American and Arabic influences, with more spices, including cumin, paprika and dried chillies, than the Spanish norm.

As on the other islands, the staple product par excellence is *gofio* (pictured, above left), toasted grain that takes the place of bread and can be made sweet or savoury. The traditional *cabra* (goat) and *cabrito* (kid) remain the staple animal protein.

Feast Like a Local

A garden shed, family sitting room, empty garage...these are just a few of the typical locations where you can find *guachinches*: no-frills eateries serving home-cooked traditional meals for less than €10. Particularly prevalent in the north, and very popular at weekends, *guachinches* are difficult to find if you're not a local in the know. One way to savvy up is to download the Android or Apple app guachapp. There is also a Guachinches

de Tenerife Facebook page with regularly updated information.

Canarian Food Fair

This week-long event held in Los Cristianos in mid-March showcases food and produce from all over the Canary Islands, with free tastings and an opportunity to purchase your favourites.

Best Traditional Food

Bodeguita Canaria A local Santa Cruz haunt serving freshly made Canarian classics in a homey setting. (p49)

ANDREI BORTNIKAU/SHUTTERSTOCK ©

La Casa de Oscar La Laguna's atmospheric, packed La Casa serves traditional, well-presented dishes. (p70)

Sabor Canario An atmospheric La Orotava restaurant with a traditional patio and authentic local cuisine. (p105).

Best Contemporary Dining

Guaydil Classy but casual La Laguna restaurant with a creative, international menu and contemporary decor. (p71)

Kazan Superb and expertly presented Japanese cuisine from this dapper Michelin-starred restaurant. (p51)

Guannabi Faultless food served in a good-looking

space on Santa Cruz' La Noria. (p51)

NUB The fusion cuisine has won this stylish restaurant a Michelin star. (p71)

Tito's Bodeguita A perennially popular spot outside Puerto de la Cruz, with pretty gardens and an attached winery. (p87)

Worth a Trip: Güímar

Rural Güímar on the east coast is known for its mysterious pyramids and its excellent Canarian restarant. The rustic dininghall at **Hotel Rural Finca Salamanca** (☏ 922 51 45 30; https://en.hotel-fincasalamanca.com; set menu €14; ⏱ 1.30-4pm & 7-10.30pm Mon-Thu & Sun, to 11pm Fri & Sat) offers an excellent menu of Canarian dishes. The menu often changes, but expect treats such as *estofado de pollo con arroz* (chicken stew with rice), *atún a la plancha con papas arrugadas y mojo* (grilled tuna with wrinkly potatoes and *mojo*, a Canarian spicy sauce; pictured above right), and *lasaña de verduras* (vegetable lasagne).

Green Spaces

Tenerife has some truly lovely parks and green spaces, particularly around Puerto de la Cruz. The gardens here are truly diverse; some have a tangible sense of English gentility (with croquet lawns, no less), while others are more subtropical. Throughout the island the town parks are always family friendly, as well as being highly maintained and lushly landscaped with subtropical plants and the ubiquitous palms.

Pretty Parks

As in mainland Spain, parks and public gardens are an integral part of the infrastructure here and are much-loved focal points for local life. There's always plenty of shady seating, as well as playgrounds and, increasingly, exercise equipment for adults. Toilets are generally close to hand, as well as those other necessities: a cafe or bar. Some parks have bandstands where concerts take place, especially at fiesta time. Increasingly, parks are also showcasing sculpture, often contemporary, while others double as venues for art-and-craft markets.

Botanical Gardens

Tenerife is home to, arguably, the most stunning botanical gardens in the Canaries. They are wonderful places to while away a few hours, with the added plus of generally ensuring plenty of natural shade.

Best Natural & Rural Parks

Anaga Mountains This northeasterly region is wild and very green, with pine-clad mountains and forests of ancient laurels. (pictured above; p140)

Parque Nacional del Teide The terrain is volcanic, rather than 'green' but is still full of colour and otherworldly intrigue; come here in springtime for the wildflowers. (p134)

Best Botanical Gardens

Palmetum A vast collection of palms from around the world comprise this Santa Cruz park on the seafront. (p47)

Jardín Botánico The most famous gardens on Tenerife, with a fascinating history and some extraordinary plants and trees. (p78)

Risco Belle Aquatic Gardens A lush water garden in Puerto de la Cruz with lakes, fountains and dazzling plants and flowers. (p84)

Sitio Litre Garden While orchids are the highlight here, the rest of this garden is a well-established leafy oasis of trickling water and tranquillity. (p85)

Hijuela del Botánico A small, delightful botanical garden in La Orotava with birds, butterflies and meandering pathways. (p103)

Jardínes del Marquesado de la Quinta Roja These terraced gardens provide a cascade of colour right in the centre of La Orotava. (p101)

Best City Parks

Parque García Sanabria A delightful collection of Mediterranean and subtropical trees and flowers, interspersed with water features and sculptures. (p48)

Plaza Príncipe de Asturias Sit under the shade of a giant Indian banyan tree at this fine capital-city park. (p43)

Best Wilderness Locations

Anaga Mountains Dense forest dripping with life and draped with little-trodden hiking trails. (p140)

Parque Nacional del Teide Sure, everyone wants to come here, but it's huge, so finding remote solitude isn't hard. (p134)

Shopping

It's easy to avoid the straw donkeys and sex-on-the-beach shot glasses: the island has a chain of quality-controlled souvenir shops that champion local art and crafts. The larger towns also have a pedestrian shopping area where idiosyncratic small shops jostle for space next to national chains. Delis are fun for browsing – mojo salsas *make great gifts, as do other gourmet goodies.*

Fashion & Textiles

While there are stores devoted to the main Spanish and international designers, you can also hunt out small boutiques with homegrown talent or those specialising in ethnic or boho-chic threads. Shoes are generally a reliable buy here, good quality and usually cheaper than on the mainland. Leatherwear has also long been associated with Spain, and the Canaries have plenty of shops that sell jackets, bags and belts at highly competitive prices. Lace and embroidery are other specialities and the work is exquisite, although watch out for cheap imitations from China.

Ceramics & Jewellery

Simple terracotta pots that emulate Guanche designs are popular, along with more sophisticated ceramics and distinctive imported Spanish pottery. Silver jewellery and pearls are both relatively inexpensive. The company Tenerife Pearl advertises widely and has several outlets on the island.

Gourmet Goods

Gourmet food markets have opened in several towns and are fun, vibrant spaces where you can eat and drink, as well as shop. In addition there are small speciality stores where you can find an excellent range of jarred goodies as well as local cheese and *jamón* (ham; you can usually ask for a taste).

SALVADOR AZNAR/SHUTTERSTOCK ©

Best Food & Wine Shops

El Rincon Extremeño A La Laguna temple to all things pork-inclined, plus local cheese and gourmet goodies. (p73)

Licoreria Puerto A crammed-full space of every imaginable deli item, from chilli-spiked sauces to chocolates, in Puerto de la Cruz. (p93)

Canary Wine Small outlet in Santa Cruz with a big range of Canarian wines and a helpful owner. (p54)

Best Souvenir Shops

Casa de la Aduana A large selection of arts and crafts, as well as wine and gourmet delights, in Puerto de la Cruz. (p92)

MAIT Museum shop in La Orotava specialising in Latin American crafts, displayed in a wonderful dazzle of patterns and colour. (p106)

La Alpizpa The original and colourful crafts at this shop in Los Cristianos are made by locals with learning disabilities. (p119)

Best Fashion Boutiques

Dolores Promesas This dynamic Santa Cruz–based designer appeals to the fashionably chic with her individual styles and richly patterned fabrics. (p55)

Carey Just the spot in Puerto de la Cruz for picking up glitzy accessories or that showstopping outfit. (p93)

Tina A wonderfully eccentric Los Cristianos boutique selling serious bling. (p120)

Architecture

Tenerife is home to some of the most stunning historical architecture of the archipelago, with distinctive styles that are often combined with eye-catching effect. One of the most appealing features of the traditional building is the lavish ornamentation on the woodwork, visible in interior patios, on building facades and also evident on the painted Moorish-inspired Mudéjar (Islamic-influenced architecture) ceilings.

Canarian Architecture

Influenced mainly by Portuguese and Andalucian traditional architecture, the typical Canarian house is distinctive for being practical, first and foremost. Rooms are typically built around a central patio, generally filled with flowers and water features, and ultimately designed to create an outdoor cool living space. More-affluent homes will include a 2nd-floor shaded gallery, usually constructed of carved wood and supported by slender stone or wood columns. The facades are typically painted in shades of yellow, pink and ochre. Latticed shutters allow air to circulate while providing shade from the sun, and door and window frames carved out of natural stone provide a classic elegance to the facade.

Religious Architecture

Many of Tenerife's churches and cathedrals date back to the 15th-century Gothic period, while others include Renaissance elements, such as arches and cloisters, as well as baroque facades and entrances. Look out for the elaborate Mudéjar ceilings, which combine Christian art with Moorish patterns to stunning effect. The majority of churches here have simple whitewashed exteriors creating a distinctive island look and blending in comfortably with their surroundings.

ROSSHELEN/SHUTTERSTOCK ©

Best Contemporary Architecture

Auditorio de Tenerife A striking Santa Cruz building, designed by Spain's leading contemporary architect, Santiago Calatrava. (Pictured above; p46)

Tenerife Espacio de las Artes (TEA) All angled lines, dramatic lighting and glass, the TEA interior is a thoroughly modern space in Santa Cruz. (p36)

Parque Marítimo César Manrique Manrique is the most famous architect in the Canaries; this Santa Cruz park provides a taster of his distinctive style. (p49)

Best Historical Architecture

Museo de Bellas Artes This neoclassical former convent in Santa Cruz is decorated with busts of famous people from Tenerife's history. (p48)

Casa Torrehermosa A handsome 17th-century mansion in La Orotava with exceptional carved wooden detail. (p106)

Best Religious Architecture

Iglesia de la Concepción An icon on the La Orotava skyline and a baroque beauty with distinctive twin towers. (p101)

Iglesia de Nuestra Señora de la Concepción An exceptional Santa Cruz church dating from 1498, with a traditional Mudéjar coffered ceiling. (p47)

Catedral This imposing La Laguna cathedral exhibits several architectural styles, including neoclassical and Gothic. (p67)

For Kids

Tenerife is a favourite destination for families as there are plenty of sights and activities to keep the kiddies amused and entertained. Stripped back to basics, the beaches and virtual year-round sunshine are pretty good raw ingredients, and then there are the theme parks, camel rides, museums, parks and water sports. The culture here also celebrates children, who will be made welcome just about everywhere, including restaurants and bars.

For Free

While there are plenty of attractions designed specifically with children in mind, including theme parks and zoos, public spaces – such as town and village plazas – also morph into informal playgrounds, with children kicking a ball around, riding bikes and playing while parents enjoy a drink and tapas at one of the surrounding bars. Local children also stay up late and at fiestas it's commonplace to see even tiny ones toddling the streets at 2am.

Accommodation

Provided you are willing to share a bed with your tot, many hotels here do not impose a surcharge, although requesting a cot or extra bed will normally up the price slightly.

Best Attractions

Parque Marítimo César Manrique A vast watery playground in Santa Cruz with several pools, including those with shallow depths for toddlers. (p49)

Lago Martiánez A Manrique creation, geared towards families and splashing kids, in Puerto de la Cruz. (pictured above; p86)

Siam Park A huge watery wonderland with a Thai theme that's an adventure playground for tots. (p126)

Observatorio del Teide Older children will get a kick out of having a chance to stargaze through a mammoth telescope in Parque Nacional del Teide. (p136)

Roques de García The first stretch of the walk in Parque Nacional del Teide from the car park to these extraordinary rock formations is suitable for strollers. (p135)

Best Museums

Museo de la Naturaleza y el Hombre These exhibits in Santa Cruz of reptiles,

NITO/SHUTTERSTOCK ©

birds and, in particular, bugs should fascinate children of all ages. (p38)

Museo de la Historia de Tenerife Kids may want to bypass the main exhibits and head straight for the fairy-tale carriages out back. (p62)

Museo de la Ciencia y el Cosmos Fascinating science museum in La Laguna with exhibits for children of all ages. (p68)

Best Water Sports

Neptuno A dolphin-spotting boat trip in Los Cristianos usually goes down well with kids. (p126)

Travelin' Lady This Los Cristianos outfit organises longer boat trips with whale-watching (and food; p115).

Club de Buceo An excellent Los Cristianos diving company offering courses for kids. (p115)

Family Travel: What to Bring

Although you may want to bring a small supply of items you are used to having back home (particularly baby products), Tenerife is likely to have everything you will need. Even in an emergency situation (ie running out of nappies!), there will always be one pharmacy nearby that remains open 24 hours, wherever you are staying on the island. For further information about travelling with children, check out lonelyplanet.com/family-travel or www.familytravel.com

Drinking

Whether you are seeking a superb cup of coffee, a killer cocktail or just a long cold cerveza (beer) at a terrace bar, Tenerife has a multitude of choices. Terrace bars are probably where you'll spend a lot of your time and, with such an intoxicating combination of feel-good factors, what's not to like?

SALVADOR AZNAR/SHUTTERSTOCK ©

Tenerife Tipples

The wine of Tenerife isn't well known internationally, but it's starting to earn more of a name for itself. The best-known, and first to earn the Denominación de Origen (DO) grade, which certifies high standards and regional origin, is the red Tacoronte Acentejo.

For those who prefer beer, Dorada, brewed in Santa Cruz de Tenerife, is a smooth pilsner. If you're driving, an alcohol-free version can be found.

Choosing Your Coffee

What you need to know for your daily brew: *café con leche* is about 50% coffee, 50% hot milk; *sombra* is similar, but heavier on the milk; *café solo* is a short black coffee (or espresso); *cortado* is an espresso with a splash of milk; and *cortado de leche y leche* is an espresso with condensed and normal milk.

Best Local Bars

Bar 7 Vies This La Laguna bar is superpopular with the local business bunch. (p72)

Bar Gavota Still retaining its local, beer-quaffing charms in the heart of Los Cristianos. (p118)

Bar Benidorm Traditional decor, Spanish ales on tap and a vibrant atmosphere. (p72)

Best Cafes

La Casita A charming, small Santa Cruz cafe and bar with old-world decor and gorgeous buttery cakes. (p52)

Ebano Café Long-standing and elegant cafe in Puerto de la Cruz with terrace seating and a relaxed vibe. (p88)

Café Palmelita This Santa Cruz cafe has superb pastries and opportunities to people-watch on the city's main shopping drag. (p49)

For Free

IGOR EMMERICH/GETTY IMAGES ©

Whether you're hitting the theme parks with kids in tow or trawling the cultural hotspots and museums, having this much fun on holiday can seriously cost. The good news is that there are plenty of sights and experiences here that won't cost you a céntimo.

Free Walks

Some tourist offices offer free guided town walks (in La Laguna, for example), typically covering the main sights and, where appropriate, historic centre. Sometimes these have the added bonus of allowing you to peek into places normally closed to tourists. These walking tours are not always widely advertised, so be sure to check at the respective tourist office whether and when they are being offered. Occasionally there may be a minimal charge.

Free Days

There seems to be no hard-and-fast rule but many museums and sights have a free day each month (often the first Sunday), while others may have a time period during which there is no charge for visitors. Check their respective websites.

Best Free Art & Culture

Tenerife Espacio de las Artes (TEA) Visit the fantastically designed library downstairs and admire the very cool architecture. (p36)

Churches Unless they contain sacred art museums, most churches around the island are free to enter and peruse their often very ornate interiors. (p47)

Best Free Museums

Museo de Bellas Artes A superb Santa Cruz art gallery in a sumptuous setting, with works by smock-and-beret masters such as Bruegel and Ribera. (p48)

Parque Nacional del Teide Administrative Offices Excellent and highly informative displays in La Orotava on the geology and history of El Teide. (p103)

Sports & Activities

LUIS MIGUEL SAEZ/SHUTTERSTOCK ©

True: if it's the height of summer, you may not feel like shifting far from the (beach) bar stool or sunbed but, at other times, it's good to know that there are plenty of activities available, ranging from the obvious gentle breaststroke in the sea to those that involve a backpack with muesli bars and several litres of water.

On Land

When you are virtually guaranteed perfect weather for 12 months of the year, you need to be out in the open. Hiking or walking is the most popular activity here and there is plenty of choice, ranging from gentle seafront strolls to adrenaline-fuelled ravine hikes, as well as climbs up Mt Teide. Alternatively, several world-class golf courses can help you practise your swing. Beaches in the larger resorts generally have a volleyball net and a game going on, while tennis clubs are quite plentiful. Throughout the resorts, the seafront is a fine setting for a jog or a spin, with the norm of a bike lane separate from traffic and pedestrians. Tenerife is also a major destination for cyclists, with roads of varying difficulty, from easy to punishing.

Best Water Sports

Travelin' Lady A long-standing and reputable Los Cristianos operator specialising in whale-watching tours. (p115)

K-16 Surf You can rent a board or take a class (or both) at this serious surf school in Playa de las Américas. (p127)

Neptuno There are plenty of boat-tour choices with this Playa de las Américas outfit, including one with food, drink and whale-spotting. (p126)

Club de Buceo This Los Cristianos operator has a vast range of diving courses, such as 'try dives' for absolute beginners. (p115)

Museums & Art

After decades under the dictatorship of General Franco, art and culture now have a very real presence in Tenerife, and museums throughout the island showcase local works of art, as well as history, archaeology, crafts and other aspects of the lifestyle and culture here. Museums are often located in stunning historical buildings that can be just as fascinating as the exhibits.

DAVID HERRAEZ CALZADA/SHUTTERSTOCK ©

Best Art Galleries

Tenerife Espacio de las Artes (TEA) World-class contemporary-art museum in Santa Cruz, showcasing a regular line of challenging, temporary exhibitions. (p36)

Museo de Bellas Artes A former Santa Cruz convent houses this collection of fine masters from the Flemish and Spanish schools. (p48)

Fundación Cristino de Vera This delightful small gallery in La Laguna is dedicated to the work of the late local artist Cristino de Vera. (p69)

Museo de Arte Contemporáneo This Puerto de la Cruz collection includes fine works by Óscar Domínguez and César Manrique. (p85)

Best Museums

Museo de Artesanía Iberoamericana This La Orotava museum takes a look at the fascinating link between the Canaries and the Americas. (p102)

Museo de la Naturaleza y el Hombre A cracking museum in the capital with exhibits ranging from volcanoes to archaeology, butterflies and birds. (p38)

Museo de la Historia de Tenerife An eclectic collection of exhibits housed in a fittingly period building in La Laguna. (pictured above; p62)

Museo de la Ciencia y el Cosmos Great science museum in La Laguna for kids of all ages, with plenty of hands-on exhibits and displays. (p68)

Museo Arqueológico Well laid-out displays chronicle the history of the island from the time of the Guanches. (p86)

Four Perfect Days

Day 1

Start your tour in **Santa Cruz** (p35), fawning over the classical works in the **Museo de Bellas Artes** (p48), before admiring the outdoor charms of the **Parque García Sanabria** (pictured; p48).

Size up the astonishing contemporary architecture of the **Tenerife Espacio de las Artes** (TEA; p36), the island's breathtaking modern-art gallery, and then head off to learn about life many moons ago at the **Museo de la Naturaleza y el Hombre** (p38).

Finish your day in the capital with a stroll to the **Auditorio de Tenerife** (p46) or the nearby **Palmetum** (p47), then hop on the tram to **La Laguna** (p61) to enjoy an evening hitting the clubs and bars in the vibrant student *barrio* (district) of **El Cuadrilátero** (p72).

Day 2

On day two, spend the morning looking at the sumptuous colonial-style buildings and fascinating sights in **La Laguna** (p61), then grab yourself a table at **La Casa de Oscar** (p70) restaurant for a lunchtime Canarian feast.

Once you've had your fill, jump on a bus to **Puerto de La Cruz** (p77). Explore the centre and enjoy an afternoon coffee-and-cake break at **Ebano Café** (p88) overlooking the picturesque church.

Walk off all that sweet stuff at the crowning glory of Puerto, the **Jardín Botánico** (p78). When you've made room for some dinner, head for the neighbourhood of **La Ranilla** (pictured; p81) to browse the menus of Puerto's hippest eateries.

Day 3

On the third day, grab breakfast on the run from one of the bakeries in pretty **La Orotava** (p95), then poke your head high above the clouds in the stunning **Parque Nacional del Teide** (pictured; p134).

The fit and fearless can make an all-day hiking assault on the summit (advance bookings are needed); the fearless but not so fit can take it easy in the cable-car ride to just below the peak.

Everyone can enjoy the easy but terrific walk around the **Roques de García** (p135). Once you've tackled Teide, hit the road south towards **Los Cristianos** (p109), and head to the long-established **El Cine** (p116) for a much-deserved seafood dinner.

Day 4

Start your day at **Puerto de Los Cristianos** (p110) and take a look at the kiosks advertising water sports and seafaring trips, including whale-watching and deep-sea fishing. Make a decision for later in the day, then have breakfast at **Sopa** (p117)

Head for the old town and a peruse of the shops. Pop into **Librería Barbara** (p120) for a browse through the excellent range of multilingual books.

Spend the afternoon on one of the sandy beaches, such as Playa del Duque (pictured; p126), then head for a night out in **Playa de las Américas** (p130). There is no shortage of nightlife in this part of town, ranging from sophisticated **Papagayo** (p130) to Irish pubs, live music and a more raucous choice of Brit-run bars.

Need to Know

For detailed information, see Survival Guide p143

Language
Spanish

Currency
Euro (€)

Visas
No visa required for citizens/residents of EU and Schengen countries, or for tourist visits of up to 90 days for citizens/residents of Australia, Canada, Israel, Japan, NZ and USA.

Money
ATMs are widely available and credit cards are accepted in most businesses.

Mobile Phones
Buy a pay-as-you-go mobile with credit from €30. Local SIM cards can be used in unlocked GSM phones.

Time
Greenwich Mean Time (GMT/UTC), plus an hour in summer for daylight-saving time.

Tipping
Small change in restaurants; round up to the nearest euro in taxis.

Daily Budget

Budget: Less than €100

Dorm bed: €20–25

Double room in a budget hotel: €40–75

Pizza or pasta: €6–15

Bus tickets: €5–10

Midrange: €100–200

Double room in a hotel: €80–100

Lunch and dinner in local restaurants: €25–45

Admission to sights: €5–15

Taxi trips: €10–15

Top End: More than €200

Double room or suite in a hotel: €150–200

Lunch and dinner with wine in a high-end restaurant: €50–100

Admission to sights: €15–20

Theatre ticket: €18

Advance Planning

Three months before Reserve your accommodation early, especially for the southern resorts.

One month before Buy tickets online for world-class performances at Santa Cruz de Tenerife's Auditorio de Tenerife and make reservations for the best restaurants.

One week before Reserve a place in advance for climbing to El Teide's summit: if you allow a week you'll be likely to get a space.

Arriving in Tenerife

Most travellers to Tenerife will arrive via air. Two airports serve the island: **Tenerife Sur** (Reina Sofía; 📞922 75 95 10; www.aena.es) and **Tenerife Norte** (Los Rodeos; 📞902 40 47 04, 922 63 56 35; www.aena.es)

✈ Tenerife Sur Airport

About 20km east of Playa de las Américas; handles international flights.

✈ Tenerife Norte Airport

Located near Santa Cruz in the north of the island; handles almost all interisland flights (plus a few international and mainland services).

Getting Around

Tenerife has a comprehensive public-transport system.

🚌 Bus

TITSA (www.titsa.com) runs an efficient spider's web of bus services all over the island, as well as within Santa Cruz and other towns.

🚗 Car

Car-hire agencies are plentiful and you shouldn't have a problem getting a vehicle, even if you want same-day rental.

🚕 Taxi

You can take a taxi anywhere on the island but it is an expensive way to get around.

Fishing boats, Santa Cruz de Tenerife (p35)

Tenerife Regions

Puerto de la Cruz (p77)
A gracious resort town with top-notch restaurants, tapas bars and nightlife, plus beaches for swimming and a leafy central plaza.

La Orotava (p95)
One of the prettiest towns on Tenerife, with great souvenir shopping and traditional restaurants and bars.

Jardín Botánico

⊙ *Garachico*

Casa de los Balcones

Playa de las Américas & Costa Adeje (p123)
A buzzing nightlife and some of the island's top restaurants and hotels make this one of the most popular stretches of coastline for tourists.

⊙ *Parque Nacional del Teide*

Los Cristianos (p109)
Superb beaches and lots of sights and activities for children make this one of Tenerife's top family destinations.

Tenerife Sur (Reina Sofía) Airport

⊙ *Puerto de Los Cristianos*

Museo de la Historia de Tenerife

Anaga Mountains

Tenerife Norte
(Los Rodeos)
Airport

**Museo de la Naturaleza y el Hombre;
Tenerife Espacio de las Artes (TEA);
Mercado de Nuestra Señora de África**

Santa Cruz de Tenerife (p35)
The Canarian capital in every sense with great shops, restaurants and sights.

*Atlantic
Ocean*

La Laguna (p61)
A fascinating Unesco World Heritage town famed for its compelling historic architecture and sights, with a lively student geared nightlife.

Explore
Tenerife

Worth a Trip 🔭

Tenerife's Walking Tours 🥾

Tenerife's Driving Tours 🚗

Garachico (p138) CRISTIAN BALATE/SHUTTERSTOCK ©

Explore ⊛
Santa Cruz
de Tenerife

Whatever you do, don't bypass the bustling capital, the handsome and friendly port of Santa Cruz, in your dash for the beach. Backing onto a superb range of undulating hills, this wholly Spanish city is home to grand architecture, sophisticated shops, a terrific spread of quality restaurants, riveting museums and art galleries, and a tropical oasis of birdsong, fountains and greenery.

The Short List

○ **Tenerife Espacio de las Artes (TEA; p36)** *Checking out the magnificent architecture and art exhibitions at this contemporary space.*

○ **Auditorio de Tenerife (p46)** *Catching a performance of opera, dance or classical music, or simply admiring the arresting architecture.*

○ **Museo de la Naturaleza y el Hombre (p38)** *Meeting the mummies and learning about the island's indigenous inhabitants, the Guanches.*

○ **Mercado de Nuestra Señora de África (p40)** *Picking up a picnic at this atmospheric market.*

Getting There & Around

🚌 TITSA buses provide a city service around Santa Cruz and to the rest of the island.

🚈 A tram line (www.metrotenerife.com) links central Santa Cruz with La Laguna.

🚗 Driving around town is not very easy and not particularly necessary as the central area is not huge.

⚓ Ferries sail from the Estación Marítima Muelle Ribera.

Santa Cruz de Tenerife Map on p44

Top Experience 📷
Tenerife Espacio de las Artes (TEA)

This extraordinary modern art-museum has massively contributed to Santa Cruz' importance as a cultural capital. The architecture of this stunning contemporary building is cutting edge, with three large, light-filled galleries displaying temporary exhibitions of art, photography and installation works, including the creative output of up-and-coming Spanish artists. The design of the library downstairs is simply a knockout.

◎ MAP P44, D4

www.teatenerife.es

Avenida de San Sebastián 10

adult/child €7/free, films €4

🕙 10am-8pm Tue-Sun

Contemporary Lines

TEA's building is daring and contemporary and creates the perfect framework for the genre of contemporary art. The building was designed by the Swiss architects and Pritzker Prize Laureates Jacques Herzog and Pierre de Meuron, famed for their innovative construction, with a prestigious portfolio that includes London's Tate Modern. The dramatic triangular design here combines concrete construction with vast windows, spacious skylit galleries, abstract-designed windows to admit light, lofty greenery and dramatic contemporary lighting.

Biblioteca

Open 24 hours a day, the TEA's stunning *biblioteca* is a design beauty. This vast open-plan room has a contemporary feel. Visitors will find an uncluttered space that libraries around the world should strive to emulate. There are quiet cubicles (and sofas outside) where you can sit and read, and books and magazines for browsing, including some in English. The childrens' library is downstairs.

Cinema

The cinema at TEA (€4) is dedicated to independent, art and experimental film and documentaries, allowing you the chance to see material that may be rarely screened. All films (shown at 7pm and 9.30pm Friday to Sunday) are in their original language, with Spanish subtitles.

★ **Top Tips**

○ Take the time to explore all the installations, including finding out what's on at the cinema.

○ Parking is available across the street at the Mercado de Nuestra Señora de África.

○ The galleries are not huge, and you can often enjoy them solo if you visit early in the morning.

○ Avail yourself of the guided visits (€15).

✗ **Take a Break**

○ Next to the library downstairs, the well-named Cafetería del TEA (p52) is a handy, chilled-out and particularly snappy-looking place for a coffee and pastries.

○ Otherwise, cross the road to the Mercado de Nuestra Señora de África (p40) and head downstairs to the fish market, where several small restaurants cook up the freshest seafood in town.

Santa Cruz de Tenerife Tenerife Espacio de las Artes (TEA)

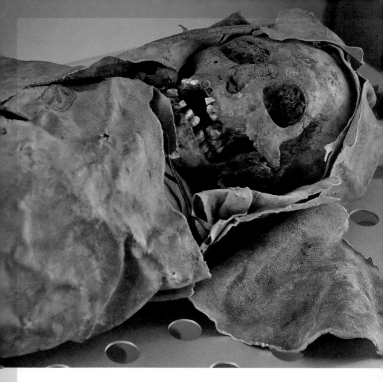

Top Experience 📷
Museo de la Naturaleza y el Hombre

This brain-bending amalgam of natural science and archaeology is one of the city's main draws, and one of the best museums in all the Canary Islands. Set inside the former civil hospital, exhibits are spread over three floors of well-lit galleries. The island's flora, fauna and geology are covered in informative displays, plus there's a section on archaeology and ethnology, including a fascinating exhibit about the Guanches' lifestyle and culture.

⊙ MAP P44, D4

www.museosdetenerife.org

Calle Fuente Morales

Admission €5

🕘 9am-8pm Tue-Sat, 10am-5pm Sun & Mon

Volcanoes

This exhibit on the ground-floor (area 1) provides the perfect introduction to the archipelago, with a giant panel noting the timescale of the islands, back to the formation of Fuerteventura 20 million years ago. The audiovisual presentation about the eruption of El Teide is a particularly powerful and mesmerising display; unlike much of the museum, most of the signage here is multilingual.

The Guanche People

The excellent exhibition on the indigenous population (2nd floor, area 1) includes a collection of prehistoric skulls neatly displayed in glass cases, along with tools, jewellery and everyday objects from daily life. There is a fascinating display of Guanche mummies and skulls with faces dried into contorted expressions (pictured). There's also an absorbing section here devoted to archaeological finds on each of the islands as well as an area displaying Berber ceramics.

Vertebrates

Touch-sensitive screens provide access to fascinating information about the birds, mammals and reptiles found on the Canary Islands (1st floor, area 5). Listen to birdsong and discover the creature that's now a threatened species, plus those that are extinct – like the lava mouse and, more happily perhaps, the giant rat. Check out the giant lizard whose mummified remains are on display.

★ Top Tips

o Access the handy online audiotour, available in six languages.

o Avoid school groups by visiting at the weekend or during the late afternoon.

o Don't rush! There is a wealth of fascinating information here; allow at least two hours for your visit.

✖ Take a Break

o The museum's classy courtyard cafe is the handiest place to have a breather, and serves a good selection of drinks, snacks and pastries.

o For a fresh fruit juice (or something stronger) and doses of people-watching, head around the corner to Mojos y Mojitos (p53), a fashionable bar with terrace seating.

Santa Cruz de Tenerife Museo de la Naturaleza y el Hombre

Top Experience 📷
Mercado de Nuestra Señora de África

This tantalising market is housed in an eye-catching building that combines a Latin American feel with Moorish-style arches and patios. A lofty clock tower helps in locating the place – or just follow the shopping baskets; the mercado offers the freshest, competitively priced produce, and is the top choice for locals, including restaurateurs. Stalls are spread over two bustling floors, with flower sellers, churros kiosks, benches and lush subtropical greenery.

◎ MAP P44, C4

Avenida de San Sebastián

🕙 9am-2pm;

🅿

Speciality Stores

Save money by buying your gourmet deli items here such as jars of spicy *mojo salsa,* cactus marmalade and local honey. On the main Patio Naciente, head for stalls such as Mi Mundo Gourmet (p56), which sells and has tastings of cheese and *jamón* (ham); **Herboristeria Mil Variedades** (Patio Naciente; ⊗7.30am-3pm), specialising in medicinal herbs for every imaginable ailment; or **Il Gelato del Mercado** (Gelato €1-3; ⊗9.30am-3pm Tue-Sun; 🐾), for a mouthwatering selection of gelato, served in crispy cones or small tubs. For fresh fish, head downstairs to the fish market.

Architecture

The *mercado* was built in the early 1940s (look for the plaque near the rear entrance). This was a time when architects had abandoned *modernismo* and turned towards a more vernacular architectural style. Unlike traditional markets, stalls are organised around a flower-festooned central patio, which is a meeting-and-greeting place for locals as well as a venue for concerts.

Local Wine

Look for Canary Wine (p54). The owner has a wealth of knowledge and will provide you with information about local wines, including eco-wines and the renowned banana wine, which costs just €8 a bottle. The Lambrusco-style rosé *viña norte* is also popular. It's possible to organise a tasting there and then, but it's best to book ahead if you're a group.

★ Top Tips

o There's free parking underneath the market.

o Note that prices are set; this is not a market where you barter.

o If you want to take photos of the stallholders, ask permission first and, better still, buy something from them.

o There's an excellent children's playground.

✗ Take a Break

o At **Cafetería La Terraza** (📞620 12 67 10; Patio Naciente; mains €6-8; ⊗7.30am-3pm) you can join the bleary-eyed stallholders here for their first caffeine fix of the day, and enjoy the early-morning market bustle at the adjacent fruit-and-vegetable stall.

o If it's later, head downstairs to the fish market, where you can find several small restaurants cooking up the catch of the day and fresh seafood.

Walking Tour 🥾

A Taste of Traditional Santa Cruz

Given that Tenerife's capital is a typical Canarian working city, rather than a dedicated tourist destination, getting a taste of what makes Santa Cruz tick is essentially as easy as exploring the plazas and backstreets with their local bars, parks and family-owned shops. The following route should give you a head start.

Walk Facts

Start Plaza Príncipe de Asturias

End La Tasca

Length 2km; 1½ hours

❶ Plaza Príncipe de Asturias

Pick up a coffee at traditional **Kiosco Príncipe** (p52) in the Plaza Príncipe de Asturias' subtropical park, which dates from the mid-1800s. Admire in the award-winning sculpture, *Courage*, by Hanneke Beaumont, and don't miss the traditional bandstand and fountain, and the towering trees, including Indian laurels brought over from Cuba.

❷ Plaza España

The emblematic plaza itself is at the heart of the city. Ponder the memorial to locals who died during the Spanish Civil War, take a paddle in the vast wading pool, then duck down to the tiny underground **Castillo de San Cristóbal** (☎922 28 56 05; Plaza España; ⊙10am-6pm Mon-Sat) to see fragments of the former castle that once sat majestically here.

❸ Dining with History

Weave your way through the backstreets to **La Hierbita** (☎922 24 46 17; www.lahierbita.es; Calle Clavel 19; mains €9-14; ⊙noon-10.30pm) – the first restaurant to be licensed here in 1893, in the (then) heart of the red-light district. Part of the building used to be a brothel, but there's nothing seedy about the excellent contemporary-style Canarian cuisine served here now.

❹ Traditional Cafe Charms

The delightful **Café Palmelita** (p49) has a venerable exterior and interior. The emphasis here is on indulgence: hot chocolate with double cream, or cold with vanilla ice cream; foamy frappés; buttery pastries; and traditional German cakes. It's also a great breakfast option.

❺ Calle Castillo

The main pedestrian walkway in town is lined with shops and boutiques and is the city's top see-and-be-seen street for locals on weekends. All the national chains are here, as well as smaller independent shops. Just to the south of Calle Castillo's western end, you'll find **La Tienda de Aloe Vera** (p57), which sells everything to do with this locally grown succulent.

❻ Soho

The nearby small grid of streets to the north of Calle Castillo is known as Soho and is home to some of the city's most fashionable cafes, tapas bars and shops. Next head to **La Casita** (p52), with several cosy dining rooms plus a lovely terrace.

❼ Canarian Cuisine

After a welcome respite sitting by the lily pond in the magnificent **Parque García Sanabria** (p48), head to nearby **La Tasca** (p51), one of the city's earthiest local restaurants. The decor is plain, the queues are long and the food is huge portions of hearty old-fashioned Canarian classics.

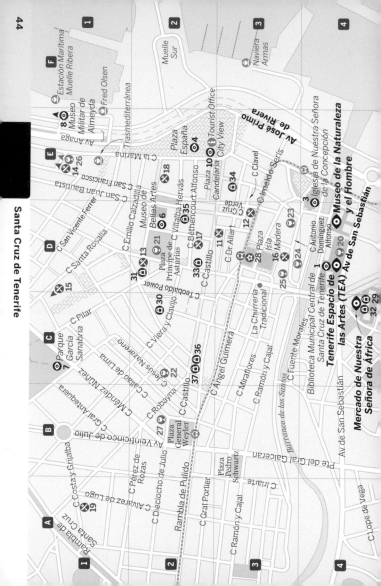

Santa Cruz de Tenerife

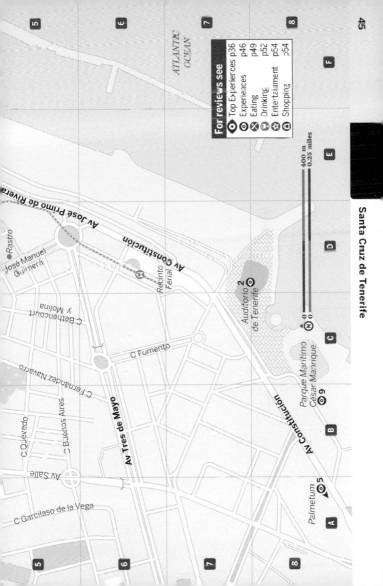

ATLANTIC
OCEAN

400 miles
0.25 miles

Av José Primo de Rivera

Rastro

José Manuel
Guimerá

Av Constitución

Recinto
Ferial

C Bethencourt
y Molina

Auditorio 2
de Tenerife

C Fomento

Parque Marítimo
César Manrique

C Fernández Navarro

Av Tres de Mayo

Av Constitución

9

C Quevedo

C Buenos Aires

Av Salle

C Garcilaso de la Vega

Palmetum
5

Experiences

Biblioteca Municipal Central de Santa Cruz de Tenerife

LIBRARY

1 👁 MAP P44, C4

This library downstairs at TEA (p36) is a design classic, a vast open-plan room with overhanging globular lights, copious natural light, angular lines and a sharp contemporary feel, all fashioned with a sense of uncluttered space that all libraries should emulate. If you're footsore, there are quiet cubicles (and sofas outside) where you can sit, read or have a snooze, and books and magazines for browsing, including some in English. A kids' library is downstairs

(www.bibliotecaspublicas.es/santa cruztenerife/informacion.htm; Tenerife Espacio de las Artes; ⏰24hr)

Auditorio de Tenerife

NOTABLE BUILDING

2 👁 MAP P44, D7

This magnificent, soaring white wave of an auditorium was designed by the internationally re-nowned Spanish architect Santiago Calatrava, and delivers shades of the Sydney Opera House, plus su-perb acoustics. Guided 45-minute tours (€7.50; reserved in advance by telephone) in English, German or Spanish take you behind the scenes of the remarkable building.

If you don't have time for a tour or to attend a performance, at least consider having a drink in the cafe

Palmetum

within the sweeping space of the main entrance. You can also walk around the entirety of the building and take plenty of arty photos to impress the folks and friends back home. (☎922 56 86 25, 922 56 86 00; www.auditoriodetenerife.com; Avenida Constitución; admission free; ⊙guided tours 10am, noon, 2pm, 4pm & 6pm; P)

Iglesia de Nuestra Señora de la Concepción CHURCH

3 ◉ MAP P44, D4

It's difficult to miss the striking bell tower of the city's oldest church, which also has traditional Mudéjar (Islamic-style architecture) ceilings. The present church was built in the 17th and 18th centuries, but the original building went up in 1498, just after Tenerife was conquered. At the heart of the shimmering silver altar is the 1494 Santa Cruz de la Conquista (Holy Cross of the Conquest), which gives the city its name.

Check out the anteroom to the sacristy. The altarpiece in the chapel beside it was carved from cedar on the orders of Don Matías Carta, a prominent personage who died before it was completed. He lies buried here and the pallid portrait on the wall was done after his death (hence the closed eyes and crossed arms). There's also a fine painting, *La adoración de los pastores (The Adoration of the Shepherds)* by Juan de Miranda. (Plaza de la Iglesia; ⊙9am-9pm Sun, mass 9am & 7.30pm)

Playa de las Teresitas

The deep honey-coloured sands of Playa de las Teresitas, 6km northeast of Santa Cruz, were imported from the Sahara. It's a lovely beach with a spectacular mountain backdrop, where the sunbathers are almost exclusively Spanish, whether local or from the mainland.

There's lots of parking available, and it's safe for children to swim here.

Plaza España SQUARE

4 ◉ MAP P44, E2

The majority of Santa Cruz' sights and museums are within easy walking distance of the revamped waterfront Plaza España, with its huge circular wading pool plus fountain that spouts four times a day (indicating high and low tides). The pool makes for excellent photographs in the early morning or late afternoon, with the architecture reflected in the water.

Santa Cruz de Tenerife's primary shopping area, pedestrianised Calle Castillo, is just west of here.

Palmetum GARDENS

5 ◉ MAP P44, A8

Conscientiously established on a former landfill area, this excellent 12-hectare botanical garden has the most diverse collection of palm trees in Europe, with specimens imported from all over the world. A detailed map leaflet helps in identifying the trees, as does signage. It's a peaceful place for a wander, with strategically placed benches for contemplating the seamless sea views.

The central octagon is a shaded walled space with volcanic rock waterfalls designed to accommodate the more delicate species, including climbing palms from Yucatán. (www.palmetumtenerife. es; Avenida Constitución; adult/child €6/2.80, joint ticket with Parque Marítimo César Manrique €7.30/3.30; ⊙11am-1pm & 4-8pm Tue-Sun; P)

Sculpture City

In 1974 Santa Cruz hosted an international street-sculpture exhibition with leading works by iconic masters of the art such as Henry Moore, Joan Miró and Óscar Domínguez. Today you can enjoy these world-class sculptures while strolling around the city. Check at the tourist office for details on specific sculpture tours departing from the beautiful Parque García Sanabria, where several of the works are on permanent display. The city also has a flourishing street-art scene, adding splashes of colour to even the most casual of wanders about town.

Museo de Bellas Artes

MUSEUM

6 MAP P44, D2

Founded in 1900 and formerly part of the adjacent church (note the fabulous stained glass), this excellent museum has an eclectic collection of paintings by mainly Spanish, Canarian and Flemish artists, including Ribera, Sorolla and Bruegel. There's also sculpture, including a Rodin, and temporary exhibitions. The massive battle-scene canvases by Spanish painter Manuel Villegas Brieva are particularly sobering. Note that the galleries are accessed via several flights of stairs, and there's no elevator. (📞922 60 94 46; www. santacruzdetenerife.es; Plaza Príncipe de Asturias; free; ⊙10am-8pm Tue-Fri, to 3pm Sat & Sun Oct-Jun, 10am-8pm Tue-Fri, to 2pm Sat & Sun Jul-Sep)

Parque García Sanabria

PARK

7 MAP P44, C1

On the northern fringe of the city centre, this park is a delightful collection of Mediterranean and subtropical trees and flowers, interspersed with sculptures, wide paths and various water features. It's the perfect place for a picnic in the shade of an Indian banyan tree or a lazy afternoon immersed in birdsong. A pleasant cafe rounds out a welcoming picture. (Calle Méndez Núñez)

Museo Militar de Almeyda

MUSEUM

8 👁 MAP P44, E1

This museum explains the military history of the islands and the successful defence of the city, brought alive by a superb 30m scale model of the flagship *Theseus*. The most famous item here, however, is *El tigre* (The Tiger), the cannon that reputedly blew off Admiral Nelson's arm when he attacked Santa Cruz in 1797. (Calle San Isidro 1; free; ⏱10am-2pm Tue-Sat)

Parque Marítimo César Manrique

SWIMMING

9 👁 MAP P44, B8

Located right off the city's main *avenida* is this park, where you can have a dip in one of the wonderful designer pools or collapse on a sunlounger and drink in the beautiful view and something refreshing. It's suitable for all ages, and great for children. Kids aged under three get in free. (📞657 65 11 27; www.parquemaritimosantacruz.es; Avenida Constitución; adult/child €2.50/1.50, joint ticket with Palmetum adult/child €7.30/3.30; ⏱10am-7pm summer, to 6pm winter)

City View

BUS

10 👁 MAP P44, E2

These double-decker open-top hop-on, hop-off buses run a 40-minute circuit around town. Setting off from and returning to Plaza de España, they take in 15 Santa Cruz sights. There's also a small City View tourist train (9.30am to 6.40pm), also running from Plaza de España, that makes seven stops. There's free entry to a number of sights, including the Palmetum, with your bus-tour ticket.

An audio guide is available in 14 languages. (📞647 30 87 76; www.tenerifecityview.com; adult/child €22/14; ⏱first/last bus 9.30am/6.30pm)

Eating

Café Palmelita

CAFE €

11 🍴 MAP P44, D3

This delightful cafe has a vintage exterior, a theme which continues within, and was founded in the late 1960s with German origins. The emphasis is on serious indulgence, with hot chocolate with double cream, or cold with vanilla ice cream; foamy frappés; buttery pastries; and traditional German cakes. All designed to put a contented waddle in your step. It's also a superb breakfast spot.

Join most of the coffee-quaffers sitting outside reading or people-watching. (📞922 88 89 04; www.palmelita.es; Calle Castillo 9; cakes €2.50-4; ⏱9am-9.30pm Mon-Fri, 9.30am-9.30pm Sat & Sun)

Bodeguita Canaria

CANARIAN €

12 🍴 MAP P44, D3

This terrific local favourite has an earthy, traditional atmosphere, with chunky dark furniture and charmingly dated decor. Try local dishes such as *ropa vieja* (literally 'old clothes'), a tasty meat-based stew with chickpeas, vegetables and potatoes, or *huevos rotos con chorizo* (scrambled eggs with chorizo). The desserts are similarly heart-warmingly homely and include *torrijas,* the Spanish take on bread-and-butter pudding.

Vegetarians may want to look elsewhere, however. (📞922 29 32 16; www.bodeguitacanaria.com; Calle Imeldo Serís 18; mains €8-10, set menu €19-25; ⏰1-4pm & 8-11.30pm Mon-Sat)

Pastelería Díaz
BAKERY €

14 🚫 MAP P44, D2

The superb pastries are what keep customers flocking back to this utilitarian-looking orange-themed place with a big reputation. The mini-*bocadillos* (sandwiches),

macaroons, *petit choux de chocolate* (eclairs), *pionono* pastries and coffees are all excellent, while the location just north of Plaza Príncipe de Asturias makes it an appealing snack spot while exploring town. (Calle Valentín Sanz 37; snacks from €1; ⏰8.30am-9.15pm Mon-Sat, 9am-9.15pm Sun)

Burger Mel
VEGAN €

14 🚫 MAP P44, E1

Keeping Santa Cruz vegans happy since 1985, though parked rather incongruously along Calle la Marina, this neat and long, white restaurant serves scrummy vegan burgers with fries and vegan mayo. Round things off with a delightful *arroz con leche* (rice pudding; €2.50) or *gofio con leche* (ground,

Parque García Sanabria (p48)

roasted grain with milk; €2.50) from the chiller.

If passing by you can grab a hummus sandwich or a vegan sobrasada sandwich from the fridge. There are two more central branches in town, and one in La Laguna too. (Calle la Marina 73; burgers €3; 🕐12.30-11pm Sun-Thu, to 11.30pm Fri & Sat; 🖊)

La Tasca
CANARIAN €

15 🍴 MAP P44, D1

The cultural and culinary opposite to the all-day English breakfasts of Tenerife's southern resorts, this neighbourhood institution makes no allowances for confused foreigners. The laughably cheap lunch menus mean there's often a queue of locals waiting for the food, which consists of huge portions of sturdy Canarian classics. (🕿922 28 07 64; Calle Dr Guigou 18; mains €7-13, menú del día €7; 🕐noon-3.45pm & 8-11.45pm Mon-Sat Sep-Jul)

Guannabi
SPANISH €€

16 🍴 MAP P44, D3

The excellence of this handsome restaurant is defined not just by its superb ambience and faultless service, but by its simply supreme menu. Guannabi pulls out all the stops: the focus is on rice dishes, all perfectly executed, but the entire selection is outstanding and even the aubergine starter is a feast of flavour and smooth texture. (🕿922 87 53 75; Calle Antonio Domínguez Alfonso 34;

mains €13-26; 🕐1-11pm Sun-Thu, to 11.45pm Fri & Sat)

El Lateral 27
CANARIAN €€

17 🍴 MAP P44, D2

Jovial and welcoming staff, happy shoppers and a menu of tried and tested local dishes make this place a perennial favourite. Offerings like oxtail (or goat) stew, suckling lamb shoulder and seafood pie are crowd-pleasers, while a decent choice of vegetable dishes keeps vegetarians happy. (Calle Bethencourt Alfonso 27; mains €10-15; 🕐7am-midnight Mon-Sat; 🖊)

Kazan
JAPANESE €€€

18 🍴 MAP P44, E2

Kazan's Michelin star has assured it a large fan base in town and far beyond. The setting: lightly polished wood and beige fabric chairs, muted and understated yet stylish. The food: the freshest ingredients coaxed into beautifully formed, delightful Japanese presentations. If in doubt, aim for the daily suggestions. The name Kazan and the kanji 火山 on the door simply mean 'Volcano'. Reserve. (🕿922 24 55 98; www.restaurantekazan.com; Paseo Milicias de Garachico 1; tasting menu €75; 🕐1.30-3.30pm Mon-Sat & 8.30-11pm Tue-Sat)

El Aguarde
CANARIAN €€€

19 🍴 MAP P44, A1

This special-occasion place, exuding a minimalist elegance to accompany its finely crafted

Churros & Chocolate

You could conceivably sit outside, but the nearby traffic at **La Churreria Tradicional** (Map p44, D3; Calle Valentín Sanz 3; churros €1.70; ⏱7am-1pm Mon-Sat, to 12.30pm Sun) is a bit snarly. Instead, head inside and join the locals in ordering up filling servings of churros and delicious mugs of hot chocolate (€1.70). A meal in itself: choose your churros (€1.70), either *gruesos* (thick) or *finos* (thin), then sit back and enjoy.

dishes, gets rave reviews. The menu changes according to what is fresh and in season, but includes a good selection of meat and fish dishes (black rice and squid, crayfish croquettes) and at least one vegetarian choice. Desserts are exquisite; try the lemon mousse with *cava* (sparkling wine) and mint. (📞922 28 91 42; www.restauranteelaguardetene rife.es; Calle Costa y Grijalba 21; mains €15-25; ⏱1-4pm Mon, 1-4pm & 9-11pm Tue-Sat; 🛜)

Drinking

Cafetería del TEA   CAFE

20 🚇 MAP P44, D4

Overhung by globular lights and defined by the crisp and stylishly neat lines of its stainless-steel and grey-cloth furniture, this

space downstairs in Tenerife Espacio de las Artes (p36) is an excellent choice for a dose of minimalist design to go with your coffee and pastries. It's open until 9pm, making it a good choice for the evening. (Tenerife Espacio de las Artes; TEA); ⏱8am-9pm Mon-Fri, 10am-9pm Sat & Sun; 🛜)

Kiosco Príncipe   CAFE

21 🚇 MAP P44, D2

Grab a coffee at this traditional kiosk located in the subtropical park of Plaza Príncipe de Asturias, which dates to the mid-1800s. Admire the award-winning sculpture *Courage* by Hanneke Beaumont, the traditional bandstand and fountain, and the lofty shade-providing trees, including Indian laurels imported from Cuba. It's always full of local strollers, with plenty of bench space to watch the comings and goings. (Plaza Príncipe de Asturias; ⏱8am-7pm Mon-Fri, to 3pm Sat)

La Casita   CAFE

22 🚇 MAP P44, C2

Managed by a fashionable young team, but themed like grandma's country cottage with an array of cuckoo clocks and ancient bits and bobs, this enticing cafe sports original tilework and several cosy dining rooms plus a lovely terrace upstairs for sinking a beer. There are also simple lightweight mains like salads, burgers and croquettes, plus delicious cakes and pies. (📞922

24 78 51; Calle Jesús Nazareno 14; 🕐10am-midnight Tue-Sat; 🕿)

GastroMag Café
CAFE

If you can't attend a concert or fit in a tour at Auditorio de Tenerife (see 2 🔘 Map p44, D7), then at the very least you can immerse yourself in the interior architecture by stopping here for a coffee or drink, if not breakfast, brunch or lunch. The food, such as wraps and burgers, is less exclusive than you would expect in such a setting.

Seats on the terrace looking out over the glossy water are lovely in the late afternoon sun. (Auditorio de Tenerife, Avenida Constitución; snacks €3.50-6; 🕐9am-7.30pm Sun-Thu, to midnight Fri & Sat; 🕿)

La Buena Vida
BAR

23 🚍 MAP P44, D3

Snag a table on the pavement, order one of the moreish and very well-priced strawberry or peach mojitos and gaze down to the soul-stirring bell tower of the Iglesia de Nuestra Señora de la Concepción. La Buena Vida is a good place for interesting nibbles too, or for something more substantial opt for the *menú del día*. (🕿922 24 19 13; Calle Antonio Domínguez Alfonso 10; 🕐1pm-1am)

Bulan
BAR

24 🚍 MAP P44, D3

The interior of this restaurant-bar on La Noria oozes atmosphere and history, with original richly patterned tilework, wood-clad rooms and soft moody lighting. The restaurant morphs into a popular bar and drinkers drift to the seats outside. (🕿922 27 41 16; www.bulan tenerife.com; Calle Antonio Domínguez Alfonso 35; 🕐noon-1am Sun-Wed, to 3am Thu-Sat; 🕿)

Mojos y Mojitos
BAR, CLUB

25 🚍 MAP P44, D3

This popular and laid-back place on La Noria serves decent food during the day, and at night morphs into a combination of cool cocktail bar and pulsating nightclub, with DJs and occasional live music. The mojitos are understandably good, with or without alcohol. (Calle Antonio Domínguez Alfonso 38; 🕐noon-midnight

Churros and chocolate

Streets for Sipping

The colourful cafes, restaurants and bars on Calle Antonio Domínguez Alfonso (popularly known as La Noria) – one of the oldest streets in the city – comprise the stylish hub of Santa Cruz drinking culture, while a busy contingent of bars also collects along Avenida Francisco la Roche, facing the port area.

Mon-Thu, to 3.30am Fri & Sat, 1-11.45pm Sun; 🛜)

Barbas Bar   BAR

26 🍺 MAP P44, E1

Yes guys, if you have a *barba* (beard) you will be made particularly welcome at this inviting saloon-style bar – in a strip of drinking holes – right across from the port. The emphasis, fittingly, is on imported beer, with a vast choice ranging from Crabbie's Original to Corona. There's a good atmosphere and occasional live music to enjoy. (Calle la Marina 9; ⏱6pm-2am Tue-Thu & Sun, to 3am Fri & Sat)

Bar Zumería Doña Papaya   JUICE BAR

27 🍺 MAP P44, B2

Serves delicious fresh fruit juices (€2 to €3.50), including strawberry, mango, papaya, avocado and various delectable combinations. Local workers also come here at lunchtime for a quick and simple meal. (Calle Callao de Lima 3; ⏱8am-7pm Mon-Fri, to 3pm Sat)

Entertainment

Auditorio de Tenerife   LIVE MUSIC

One of Santa Cruz' top photo ops, Tenerife's leading entertainment option has dramatically designed curved-white concrete shells capped by a cresting, crashing wave of a roof (see 2 ◉ Map p44, D7). It covers and significantly enhances a 2-hectare oceanfront site. The auditorium hosts world-class opera, dance and classical-music performances, and there's a snazzy cafe in the lobby. (📞box office 902 31 73 27; www.auditoriodetenerife.com; Avenida Constitución; 🛜)

Teatro Guimerá   THEATRE

28 ⭐ MAP P44, D3

This fabulous art deco theatre is a popular venue for highbrow entertainment, whether music or theatre. Sink a predinner libation at the nearby Bar Teatro. (📞box office 902 33 33 38; www.teatroguimera.es; Plaza Isla Madera; tickets €12-18; ⏱11am-1pm & 5-8pm)

Shopping

Canary Wine   WINE

29 🔒 MAP P44, C4

The charming and helpful owner of this shop will guide you through the local wines here, including eco-wines and the

Don't Miss: Tenerife's Carnaval Capers

Channelling a true Carnaval spirit of exuberance and mayhem, Santa Cruz' own **Carnaval** (www.carnavaltenerife.com; Feb) is a nonstop, 24-hour party-orgy. The Carnaval is no modern invention, and possibly dates back to the earliest days of the settlement. Festivities generally kick off in early February and last about three weeks. Many of the gala performances and fancy-dress competitions take place in the Recinto Ferial (fairgrounds) but the streets, especially around Plaza España, become frenzied with good-natured dusk-to-dawn frivolity.

Don't be fooled into thinking this is just a sequin-bedecked excuse to party hearty, though. It may sometimes be hard to see or believe, but there is an underlying political 'message' to the whole shebang. Under the Franco dictatorship, Carnaval was banned, but still managed to continue furtively under the name 'Winter Festival'. The Catholic Church's relationship with the fascists was another source of frustration so, when Carnaval was fully relaunched after the death of General Franco, the citizens of Santa Cruz wasted no time in lampooning the perceived sexual and moral hypocrisy of the church and the fascists. Today, you will still see a lot of people dressed for the event as naughty nuns and perverted priests, and more drag queens than bumblebees in a buttercup field. And all in the name of good, clean fun. Book your accommodation ahead – if you intend to go to bed, that is.

famous banana wine with the peeled-back price of just €8 a bottle. Another popular choice is *viña norte*, a Lambrusco-style rosé. The owner can set you up with a tasting there and then, but book ahead if you're a group. (645 16 32 59; Patio Naciente, Mercado de Nuestra Señora de África; 7.30am-3pm)

La Cabaña del Té TEA

30 MAP P44, C2

This emporium dedicated to the tea leaf has a heady array of infusions from all over the world, packed into bright containers that are neatly arrayed on shelves, as well as a nice choice of teapots. (922 27 57 89; Calle Suárez Guerra 26; 10am-2pm & 5-8.30pm)

Dolores Promesas FASHION & ACCESSORIES

31 MAP P44, D2

This Spanish designer apparently became inspired as a child by her grandfather's modest haberdashery shop near Cádiz. Her designs range from casual printed T-shirts to fabulous floaty dresses in feather-light silks. (📞922 28 97 46; www.dolores promesas.com; Calle Pilar 4; 🕙10.30am-2pm & 5.30-8.30pm Mon-Fri, 10.30am-2pm Sat)

Mi Mundo Gourmet

FOOD & DRINKS

32 🔒 MAP P44, C4

Pick up your gourmet deli items at this bustling store. Look for traditional products such as jars of chilli-spiked *mojo salsa*, cactus marmalade, local honey, olive oil, herbs and spices. (📞922 09 80 57; Patio Naciente, Mercado de Nuestra Señora de África; 🕙9am-2pm Tue-Sun)

Dédalo

JEWELLERY

33 🔒 MAP P44, D2

It may look like just another small accessory shop, but step inside to discover a galaxy of well-

---

Sunday Market

The vast rambling **Rastro** (Map p44, D5; José Manuel Guimerá; 🕙9am-3pm Sun) is held every Sunday along two parallel streets starting from Mercado de Nuestra Señora de África and running along José Manuel Guimerá to the coast. For sale is the usual mix, including cut-price underwear and handmade jewellery. It's bustling and fun.

---

displayed, dazzling and exquisite jewellery, created by such eminent Spanish and Canarian jewellers as Rosa Mendéz, Carlos Reano and the shop's namesake Dédalo. Don't miss Reano's exquisite 'Bosques del Mar' series, which combines resin, tropical woods, coral and bamboo with gold, silver and bronze. (📞922 28 59 30; Calle Valentín Sanz 14; 🕙9.30am-1.30pm & 5-7.30pm Mon-Fri, to 1.30pm Sat)

Kish Vintage Apparel

ANTIQUES

34 🔒 MAP P44, E3

At first glance this shop resembles more of a jumble sale than anything else, but take the time to browse and you will discover all kinds of gems, including antique leather suitcases, kitsch ornaments and ceramics, shirts, denim jackets and jeans, preppy jerseys, sneakers, '60s floral frocks, silk scarves, records and clunky retro costume jewellery. (www.vintagestore13.com; Calle Dr Allart 32; 🕙11am-2pm & 5-8pm Mon-Sat)

Artesencías

COSMETICS

35 🔒 MAP P44, D2

Using 100% natural vegetable oils, as well as scents, this aromatically enticing ecofriendly *perfumería* purveys beautifully packaged massage oils, body and face creams, scrubs, natural air fresheners and soaps with scrumptious-sounding ingredients like green tea, caviar and honey. (📞922 29 30 52; www.

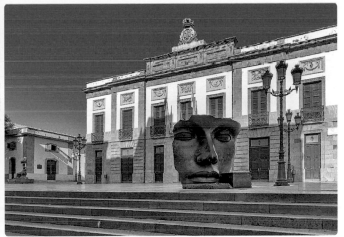

Per Adriano by Igor Mitoraj in front of Teatro Guimerá (p54)

artesencias.com; Calle Villalba Hervás 21; ⊙10am-8pm Mon-Fri, 10.30am-1.30pm Sat)

Pampling   CLOTHING

36 🔒 MAP P44, C2

Pampling sells appealing, bright, colourful, fun and tongue-in-cheek T-shirts with superb, eye-catching designs for kids and kid-dults. Fork out for a pair of Space Invaders socks – you know you always wanted to. (www.pampling.com; Calle del Castillo 63; ⊙10am-8.30pm Mon-Fri, to 8pm Sat)

La Tienda de Aloe Vera   COSMETICS

37 🔒 MAP P44, C2

Aloe vera grows prolifically throughout the Canary Islands (it was discovered in nearby North Africa) and has been recognised for its healing properties for centuries. The tiny interior of this place is stuffed full of every imaginable aloe-vera-based product from A to Z, ranging from face creams to shampoos, juices and medicinal ointments. You can buy the plants here too. (📞922 24 36 01; Calle Imeldo Serís 96; ⊙9am-1pm & 5-8pm Mon-Fri, 9am-1.30pm Sat)

Walking Tour 🚶

Holy Candelaria

Largely untouched by tourists despite being considered the holiest site in the Canary Islands, this small, atmospheric town buzzes with life, particularly on Sundays. Narrow pedestrian streets are lined with little shops selling everything from kitsch religious items to more conventional souvenirs, while the traditional tapas bars and seafood restaurants are largely geared towards a discerning local clientele.

Getting There

Candelaria is 18km south of Santa Cruz.

🚗 If you're driving, take exit 9 off the TF-1 motorway.

🚌 Buses 111, 112, 115, 116, 122, 123, 124 and 131 connect the town with Santa Cruz (€2.35, 30 minutes).

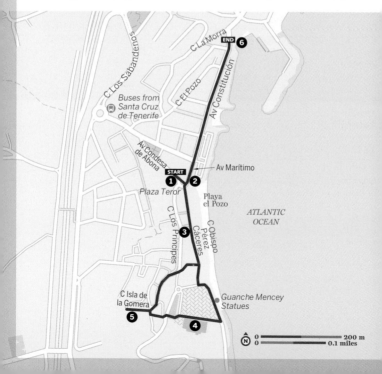

❶ Coffee Stop

If you're arriving by bus, head down to Plaza Teror via Avenida Condesa de Abona, stopping at earthy and local **Bar Mencey** (Avenida Condesa Santa María de Abona 1; snacks €2-3; 🕓6am-2am Tue-Sun) with its postage-stamp-size interior, complete with TV and slot machines. I lead to the outside terrace with slices of sea views across the way, and enjoy a strong coffee and *tostada con aceite* (toast with olive oil).

❷ Tapas Trail

Facing you is the **tourist office** (📞922 03 22 30; www.candelaria.es; Avenida de la Constitución; 🕓9am-2pm Mon-Fri), where you can grab a map and set off on one (or more!) of its five recommended Rutas de Tapas (tapas routes), to sample a variety of small dishes from various bars around town.

❸ Religious Souvenirs

Get into the soul-stirring mood by checking out the religious statues, shrink-wrapped Santa Ritas, photos, plaques, candles and holograms of the Virgin Mary at **La Casa de las Imágenes** (www. facebook.com/LaCasadelas Imagenes; Calle Obispo Pérez Cáceres 17; 🕓9.30am-8pm Tue-Sun, to 1.30pm Mon), which claims to have the largest selection of religious imagery in Spain.

❹ The Basilica

The grandiose **Basilica de Nuestra Señora de Candelaria** (🕓7.30am-7.30pm Tue-Sun, 3-7.30pm Mon; Ⓟ) sits on a vast plaza and is home to the Virgen de la Candelaria, the patron saint of the Canaries. You can't miss the nine bronze, life-size statues of the former Guanche Menceys who ruled over the island before the Spanish conquest.

❺ Local Pottery

Just past the basilica, steps lead up the right-hand side to the signposted **Centro Alferero de Candelaria** (Calle Isla de la Gomera 17; free; 🕓11am-5pm Tue-Sat), a small and very informative pottery museum. There's also a lovely shop where you buy the typical red pots, including the appealing *jarra de vino* (wine jug). There's an excellent 20-minute film that the attendant will start for you.

❻ A Fishy Lunch

Retrace your walk and follow the sea past the churros kiosks, playground and small black beach, Playa el Pozo, until you reach the harbour and **El Muelle** (Avenida Constitución 9; mains €4-16; 🕓11am-midnight), a popular seafood restaurant with a large terrace out back with harbour views that serves battered prawns, octopus vinaigrette, cuttlefish with garlic, fish of the day and tuna with *mojo* (Canarian spicy sauce).

Explore ⊛
La Laguna

The highly photogenic La Laguna is widely considered to be the most beautiful town in Tenerife. An easy day trip from Santa Cruz or Puerto de la Cruz, it has a gem of a historic town centre, with narrow poker-straight streets flanked by pastel-hued mansions, inviting bars and an idiosyncratic array of small shops.

The Short List

∘ *Museo de la Historia de Tenerife (p62)* Learning a little local history at this museum housed in a marvellous old mansion.

∘ *Catedral (p67)* Admiring the art and architecture in La Laguna's 20th-century cathedral.

∘ *Calle San Agustín (p67)* Snapping shots of pretty facades in the town's most photogenic street.

∘ *Convento de Santa Clara (p67)* Brushing up on the history of this 16th-century convent.

∘ *Tasca 61 (p70)* Sampling handmade cheese, organic meat and craft beer at this bastion of the slow food movement.

Getting There & Around

🚶 It's easy to navigate the town centre on foot.

🚌 Plenty of buses travel between La Laguna's Intercambiador Laguna Bus Station and Santa Cruz. From Santa Cruz take bus 015 (€1.45, 25 minutes).

🚃 The handy tram system (www.metrotenerife.com) also links La Laguna with Santa Cruz (€1.35, 40 minutes).

🚗 Finding a parking space on the streets of La Laguna is migraine inducing. If possible come on public transport.

La Laguna Map on p66

Historic town centre ELENA-STUDIO/GETTY IMAGES ©

Top Experience 📷
Museo de la Historia de Tenerife

Founded in 1496, La Laguna was Tenerife's original capital and attracted wealthy merchants and nobility who built their mansions here, many of which still line the narrow streets. One of the most emblematic calles (streets) is San Agustín, home to several magnificent buildings, including the excellent Museo de la Historia de Tenerife.

◉ MAP P66, D3

Casa Lercaro

www.museosdetenerife.org

Calle San Agustín 22

adult/child under 8 €5/free

🕑 9am-8pm Tue-Sat, 10am-5pm Sun & Mon

Museum Exhibits

Highlights of the collection include early
Guanche pottery and traditional crafts. Documents, maps, weapons and tools are also on
display. Other must-see items are the two
magnificent 18th- and 19th-century carriages
kept in a separate exhibition space at the rear
of the museum (open noon to 3pm): a French
rococo 18th-century Berlin and the slightly
later Landau (a carriage frequently mentioned
in Jane Austen's novels). To make the most of
your visit, download the audio guide app or
grab one of the English introductions.

Casa Lercaro

For many people, the museum building is as
fascinating as the exhibits. Dating from the
late 16th century, the mansion – with its creak-
ing floorboards, old window seats and lovely
interior patio – was built by a family of Italian
origin, hence such embellishments as the
decorative floral lintels, typical of the Genoese
Mannerism movement. The patio is complete
with a *drago* (dragon) tree and a richly carved
wooden gallery supported by stout stone
columns.

★ **Top Tips**

o Try to time your
museum visit for a
Friday and Saturday
afternoon (between
4pm to 8pm) when
there is free
admission.

o Be sure to visit the
superb gift shop at
the museum.

o Parking is a night-
mare. There's an
underground paying
car park beneath
Plaza San Cristóbal,
but if possible come
on public transport.

o Pick up the *San
Cristóbal de la La-
guna, World Heritage
Site* brochure from
the tourist office – it
maps out La Laguna's
many architectural
highlights.

✕ **Take a Break**

o Grab an outside
table at nearby Bar 7
Vies (p72), where you
can enjoy traditional
tapas, great coffee or
a long cold *cerveza*
(beer).

o Alternatively, La
Pera Limonera (p73)
is a pleasant choice
for fruit juice, coffee
or light snacks.

Walking Tour 🥾

The Flavours of La Laguna

There's a lot to like about the local lifestyle in vibrant La Laguna. Combining the sumptuous sights, student buzz, a vigorous bar scene and a beguiling mix of traditional and gourmet restaurants and markets, the town provides plenty of opportunity for visitors to get a taste of what makes the town tick.

Walk Facts

Start Pastelería Díaz
End El Cuadrilátero
Length 3km; two hours

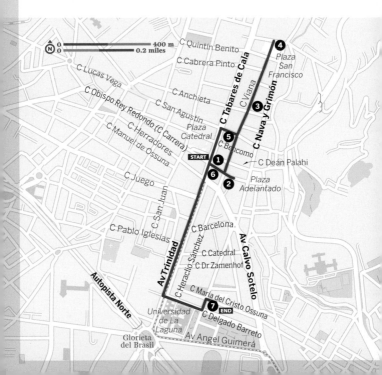

❶ Coffee & Pastry

Once voted one of the top 20 patisseries in Spain by a national newspaper, **Pastelería Díaz** (p70) may be rather unsubtle, with its blaring TV and bright-orange decor, but the pastries and coffees are superb, as attested by the inevitable queues at the door. Try the custard-filled mini-croissants.

❷ Casa de los Capitanes Generales

Make this magnificent 17th-century building your second stop. The **Casa de los Capitanes Generales** (p68) has a sumptuous inner patio, and is home to regular exhibitions and the tourist office, where you can find out what's going on, particularly any live music in El Cuadrilátero's myriad of bars.

❸ Convento de Santa Clara

Duck into the **Convento de Santa Clara** (p67) to glean something about the spiritual background of the town. There's a museum here with all kinds of priceless antiquities, but the highlight is the audiovisual presentation about the history of the nuns and how exactly they arrived in La Laguna all those decades ago.

❹ Mercado Municipal

Head to the colourful **Mercado Municipal** (Plaza San Francisco; ⏱8.30am-3pm Mon-Sat), which has close to 100 stalls, including fresh-produce counters piled high with glistening fruit and veg, and decorated by strings of garlic and bunches of fragrant herbs. This is also the place to buy the local smoked goat's cheese, fresh baked goods and flowers.

❺ Traditional Flavours

Bodegón Viana (p71) has seen little change since it first opened its doors in 1976, in both its menu and its interior. Soak up the local ambience while enjoying large servings of traditional Canarian fare and watching the local soap opera.

❻ Hot Choc

You may not want to load up with churros after your meal, but the hot chocolate at **Churrería Cafetería El Buen Paladar** (p71) is a good excuse to take a seat at a wooden table, along with the exclusively local fan base, and watch the goings-on. Don't miss the staff snipping the churros to length with scissors.

❼ El Cuadrilátero

Seize the night by the scruff and join the students who head to this rectangle of vibrant bars and clubs northeast of the university. At its heart, pedestrianised Plaza Zurita is simply two parallel lines of bars, clubs and pubs, so there's no shortage of options. Choose between chilled-out bars, whimsical drinking dens and sweaty dance-till-you-drop venues.

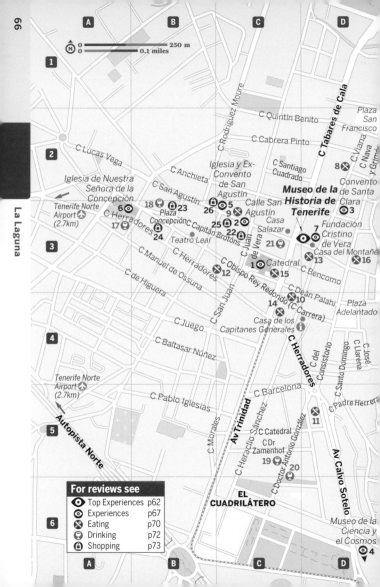

N 0 —————— 250 m
0 —————— 0.1 miles

Plaza San Francisco

C Quintín Benito

C Cabrera Pinto

C Tabares de Cala

C Rodríguez Moure

C Lucas Vega

Iglesia de Nuestra Señora de la Concepción

Tenerife Norte Airport (2.7km)

C Herradores

C Anchieta

C San Agustín

Iglesia y Ex-Convento de San Agustín

C Santiago Cuadrado

Calle San Agustín

C Viana
C Nava y Grimón

Convento de Santa Clara

Museo de la Historia de Tenerife

Casa Salazar

Fundación Cristino de Vera

Casa del Montañé

Plaza Concepción

C Capitán Brotóns

Teatro Leal

C Herradores

C Manuel de Osuna

C de Higuera

C Obispo Rey Redondo

C San Juan

C Juan de Vera

Catedral

C Bencomo

C Deán Palahí

Plaza Adelantado

Casa de los Capitanes Generales

C Carrera

C Juego

C Baltasar Núñez

C Pablo Iglesias

Autopista Norte

Tenerife Norte Airport (2.7km)

C Morales

Av Trinidad

C Barcelona

C Heraclio Sánchez

C Catedral
C Dr Zamenhof

C Doctor Antonio González

EL CUADRILÁTERO

C Herradores

C del Consistorio

C Santo Domingo

C José
C Llarena

C Padre Herrera

Av Calvo Sotelo

Museo de la Ciencia y el Cosmos

For reviews see
- 👁 Top Experiences p62
- 👁 Experiences p67
- ✖ Eating p70
- 🍷 Drinking p72
- 🛍 Shopping p73

Experiences

Catedral

CATHEDRAL

1  MAP P66, C3

Work on this magnificent cathedral was completed in 1915. A fine baroque retable in the chapel is dedicated to the Virgen de los Remedios and dates from the 16th century. Other highlights include some impressive paintings by Cristóbal Hernández de Quintana, one of the Canary Islands' premier 18th-century artists, and a splendid Carrara marble pulpit carved by Genovese sculptor Pasquale Bocciardo in 1762. An audio guide is included in the admission price. (www.catedraldelalaguna.blogspot. com.es; Plaza Catedral; €5; ⏰8am-6pm Mon-Sat, to 2pm Sun)

Calle San Agustín

STREET

2  MAP P66, C3

To see the largest number of splendid mansions standing cheek by jowl, wander along Calle San Agustín. Look for the metal plaques outside the noble facades; they have fascinating historical explanations about the buildings (in Spanish and English). Several of the buildings have been turned into offices (generally located around a grand central courtyard), which you can take a peek at.

Convento de Santa Clara

CONVENT MUSEUM

3  MAP P66, D3

Of all the convents in La Laguna, this is the most interesting,

Iglesia de Nuestra Señora de la Concepción (p69)

La Laguna's Canarian Mansions

Bright facades graced with wooden double doors, carved balconies and grey stone embellishments typify the pristinely preserved 16th- to 18th-century mansions of La Laguna, while elegant, wood-shuttered windows conceal cool, shady patios surrounded by 1st-storey verandas propped up by slender timber columns.

Calle San Agustín and the surrounding streets are lined with fine old houses. Take a look at the beautiful facade of **Casa del Montañés** (Map p66, D3; Calle San Agustín 16; ⊘10am-7pm Mon-Fri), with its decorative carved window frames. Destroyed by a fire in 2006, **Casa Salazar** (Map p66, C3; Calle San Agustín 28; ⊘10am-7pm Mon-Fri) has a beautiful, if austere, baroque facade and two lovely patios; it is now used for offices. The imposing **Casa de los Capitanes Generales** (Calle Obispo Rey Redondo 5; ⊘9am-8pm Mon-Fri, to 2pm Sat & Sun) is beside the *ayuntamiento* (town hall) and houses the tourist office. The distinctive blue facade of the mansion at Calle Carrera 66 is the former home of surrealist painter Óscar Domínguez.

Both the exterior and interior of the 19th-century **Teatro Leal** (Map p66, B3; www.teatroleal.es; Calle Obispo Rey Redondo 54; ⊘performances only) create a pleasingly over-the-top butterfly of a building that is open to the public only during performances.

Whenever you see an open door, peek inside – with luck the inner sanctum will also be open, but do remember that many are private residences or offices.

renowned for its beautiful latticework wooden balcony and cloister. The museum covers nine rooms and contains some of the most precious artworks and artefacts from the convent collection, including a magnificent 18th-century silver altar. A 10-minute audiovisual presentation (in English and Spanish) explains the fascinating history of the convent, from its founding in 1547 by 10 Franciscan nuns. (cnr Calles Anchieta & Viana; adult/child €3/free; ⊘10am-5pm Tue-Fri, to 2pm Mon)

Museo de la Ciencia y el Cosmos
MUSEUM

4 ◉ MAP P66, D6

If you enjoy pushing buttons and musing on the forces of nature, you'll have fun at this museum, which introduces key scientific concepts in an engaging and thought-provoking way. Located about 1.5km south of Plaza Adelantado and easily accessible by the tram to Santa Cruz (which stops right outside), it also has a *planetario* (planetarium), so you can stargaze during the day. (✆ 922 31 52 65; www.museosdetenerife.org; Avenida de los Menceyes 70; adult/child/student €5/free/€3.50, planetarium €1; ☺ 9am-8pm Tue-Sat, 10am-5pm Sun & Mon; P)

Iglesia y Ex-Convento de San Agustín
CHURCH

5 ◉ MAP P66, C3

This church went up in flames in 1964, lost its roof and is now out of bounds and in ruins, but you can peer through the gap in the wall at the somnolent skeletal remains and the plants busy reclaiming the abandoned stonework. The cloisters, filled with tropical plants and flowers, are open to the public and are probably the prettiest in town. The rooms surrounding the cloisters contain an art gallery of frequently changing local works. (Calle San Agustín; ☺ 10am-8pm Tue-Fri, to 3pm Sat & Sun)

Iglesia de Nuestra Señora de la Concepción
CHURCH

6 ◉ MAP P66, A3

Originally constructed in 1502, this is one of the island's earliest churches and has subsequently undergone many changes. Elements of Gothic and plateresque styles can still be distinguished, and the finely wrought wooden Mudéjar ceilings are a delight. Take a look at the font where apparently (any remaining) Guanches were traditionally

baptised, then climb the five-storey tower for stunning views of the town and beyond. Purchase tickets from the bell-tower office before entering the church. (Plaza Concepción; tower €2; ☺ tickets sold 10am-2pm Mon, to 5pm Tue-Fri)

Fundación Cristino de Vera
GALLERY

7 ◉ MAP P66, D3

La Laguna's prime arts venue houses a mixture of top-calibre temporary exhibitions as well as a permanent collection of works by acclaimed contemporary artist Cristino de Vera, who was born in Santa Cruz de Tenerife in 1931. There is also a thought-provoking audiovisual presentation about the artist and his work, which is subtitled in English. (www.fundacion-cristinodevera.com; Calle San Agustín 18; adult/child €3/free; ☺ 11am-2pm & 5-8pm Mon-Fri, 10am-2pm Sat)

Historic Tours
WALKING

To uncover the beauty of La Laguna hidden behind the city's heavy doors and walls, join one of the guided tours organised by and departing from the **tourist office** (see 1 ◉ Map p66, C3). Tours are free and in Spanish (or English, German or French with 48 hours' notice), taking in key sites and several historic buildings that cannot be visited independently.

The tour on Mondays visits the Teatro Lcal. (✆ 922 63 11 94; infoturismolaguna@aytolalaguna.es;

Town Planning

La Laguna's layout provided the model for many colonial towns in the Americas and, in 1999, it was added to the list of Unesco World Heritage sites.

Calle Obispo Rey Redondo 7; ☺tours 11.30am Mon-Fri)

Eating

Tasca 61   SPANISH €

8 🍴 MAP P66, D2

Organic, locally sourced produce, a slow-food philosophy and *artesanal* cheeses are the hallmarks of this tiny place with its limited but delicious menu of daily specials. Even the beer is locally crafted at the only ecobrewery in Tenerife: Tierra de Perros. (Calle Viana 61; mains €7-10; ☺12.30-3.30pm & 7.30-10.30pm Wed-Fri, 7.30-10.30pm Sat & Sun)

La Bourmet   BURGERS €

9 🍴 MAP P66, C3

This small and popular modern burger spot crams a lot of aroma into its small quarters, as well as a fair number of diners too, who spill out onto the seats on Calle San Agustin for doses of sun and people-watching. (Calle San Agustín 42; mains from €6; ☺1-4.30pm & 7-11pm Mon-Thu, 1-11.30pm Fri, 1-4.30pm & 7.30-11.30pm Sat, 1-4.30pm & 7.30-11pm Sun; 🛜)

Pastelería Díaz   CAFE €

10 🍴 MAP P66, C4

The bright-orange decor is a curious design choice for Pastelería Díaz, once voted one of the top 20 patisseries in Spain by a national newspaper. However, the mini-*bocadillos* (sandwiches), pastries and coffees are superb, as attested by the long-standing popularity of this place and periodic difficulty in getting a seat here. (📞922 62 62 02; Calle Obispo Rey Redondo 6; snacks €2.50-5; ☺8.30am-9pm)

Tapasté   VEGETARIAN €

11 🍴 MAP P66, D5

Come here to taste a delicious vegetarian variety of burgers, prepared several different ways, with toppings like hummus and *almogrote* (spicy cheese). They're not too pious to scrimp on desserts; try the chocolate tart with berry topping. The food is all dairy-free, with no eggs. Look for the lettuce-green painted doors. (📞822 01 55 28; www.tapaste.es; Plaza San Cristóbal 37; mains €8-12; ☺1-4pm Mon-Fri; 🖋)

La Casa de Oscar   CANARIAN €

12 🍴 MAP P66, C3

This place always has a great buzz, particularly at weekends, when the tables are packed with exuberant local families tucking into dishes like grilled tuna in coriander-spiked sauce, spicy sausage omelettes or grilled meats with *mojo* (spicy sauce). Lighter appetites can snag a barrel table and fill up fast with the Galician-style *pintxos* (tapas) lining the front bar. (☎ 922 26 52 14; Calle Herradores 66; pintxos €1.80, mains €8-10; ⊗ 8am-midnight)

Bodegón Viana   CANARIAN €

13 🍴 MAP P66, D3

Immerse yourself in the local ambience at this time-worn restaurant that has changed very little since its founding in 1976 (the menu may well be the same too...). Tuck into hearty portions of traditional Canarian dishes while catching up on the local soap opera on the corner TV. The *pescaíto frito* (fried assorted seafood) comes warmly recommended. (☎ 922 26 42 13; Calle Viana 35; mains €9-13; ⊗ 9am-1am)

Churrería Cafetería El Buen Paladar   CHURROS €

14 🍴 MAP P66, C4

This hangout with wooden tables and an exclusively local fan base is always busy. Add on those all-important La Laguna-exploring calories with a serving of churros and a thick hot chocolate, watch the staff snipping the churros with scissors, then sally forth. (☎ 922 25 80 78; Calle Tabares de Cala 2; churros €2; ⊗ 8am-1pm & 5-9pm)

Guaydil   CANARIAN €€

15 🍴 MAP P66, C3

You can't go wrong at this delightful contemporary restaurant with

its punchy, playful decor. Dishes are deftly executed, exquisitely presented and sensibly priced. One tip – if ordering a salad (recommended), ask for a half portion; the servings are huge and the staff won't object. Other typical dishes include couscous, prawn-stuffed crêpes, chicken curry and an irresistible Cuban mojito sorbet.

A kids menu (€9) is on hand for small mouths. (☎ 922 26 68 43; www.restauranteguaydil.com; Calle Deán Palahí 26; mains €10-16; ⊗ 1.30-4.40pm & 8-11.30pm Mon-Thu, 1.30-4.30pm & 8.30-11.30pm Fri & Sat; 🛜)

NUB   FUSION €€€

16 🍴 MAP P66, D3

A recent recipient of a coveted Michelin star, NUB in the La Laguna Gran Hotel works culinary wonders under the expert guidance of husband-and-wife chefs Andrea Bernadi and Fernanda Fuentes Cárdenas. Its thoughtful fusion of Canarian, Italian and Chilean flavours, perfectly presented in a set of tasting menus, are delivered in a very stylish setting. (☎ 922 07 76 06; Calle de la Nava y Grimon 18; menú €75-95; ⊗ 7-9.30pm Wed & Thu, 1.30-2.30pm & 8-10pm Fri & Sat, 1-2.30pm Sun)

Cooler Santa Cruz   ☂

If you're coming in the winter months it's worth packing a jacket or another layer, as the town is quite a bit cooler than places such as Santa Cruz.

Drinking

Bar Benidorm
BAR

17 📍 MAP P66, A3

Just what the doctor ordered, popular local drinking hole Bar Benidorm dates to 1957 and is known for its delicious *bocata de jamón* (ham sandwich), sliced fresh from one of the hefty hams curing gently above the bar (thankfully not in dense cigarette smoke these days!). The atmosphere is always bustling and locally flavoured; note the extended opening hours. (📞922 25 88 62; Plaza Dr Olivera 6; ⏰6am-1am)

Casa Viña
BAR

18 📍 MAP P66, B3

One of the best pavement settings for sipping a drink and watching La Laguna folk on the move. Within worshipping distance of the magnificent Iglesia de Nuestra Señora de la Concepción, this *vinoteca* (wine cellar) is owned

by the well-respected Viña Norte winery, based in Tacoronte. Enjoy a glass of its wine for just a couple of euros; good tapas are also available. (📞922 63 37 29; www.bodegasinsulares.es; Plaza Concepción; ⏰11am-midnight Mon-Thu, to 3am Fri & Sat; 🛜)

Bar 7 Vies
BAR

Enjoy chill-out music and a cosy interior with burgundy walls and Victoriana-style decor. Although this is more a bar than a restaurant, there are tapas and a reasonable daily menu on offer. This place (see 16 🍽 Map p66, D3) gets packed out with the local business bunch post-clock-out time. (📞922 25 73 23; Calle San Agustín 11; ⏰8am-11.30pm; 🛜)

Pub Gabbana
CLUB

19 📍 MAP P66, C5

This heaving nightclub also draws crowds of warblers and crooners for its popular karaoke nights (and contests) – just in case you feel a Whitney Houston moment coming on. It's located south of the centre in the heart of the clubbing area and is generally packed with a lively bunch of students. (📞922 00 00 00; Calle Doctor Antonio González 11; ⏰6pm-2am)

Strasse
BAR

20 📍 MAP P66, C5

Serving drinks for over 30 years, this moodily lit bar has a great range of cocktails and imported beers, plus giant-screen music

---

The Drinking Quarter

Thirsty students comprise the town's nightlife, and the bulk of the bars are concentrated in a tight rectangle northeast of the university, known as El Cuadrilátero. Plaza Zurita is pedestrianised, and made up of two rows of bars and pubs so you won't be stuck for options.

videos and an atmosphere that never misses a beat, thanks to the steady crowd of toe-tapping regulars. (☎696 55 25 93; Calle Doctor Antonio González 17; ☻6pm-2am Tue-Sat, to midnight Sun; 📶)

La Pera Limonera   JUICE BAR

21 🔂 MAP P66, C3

This convivial and contemporary tight-squeeze space is a decent choice for enjoying healthy fruit-and-veg juices or coffee. Savoury snacks and a selection of delectable sweet-tooth delights are also available. (☎922 26 71 59; Calle San Agustín 29; ☻8.30am-7.30pm Mon-Fri, 9am-2pm Sat; 📶)

Shopping

Pisaverde   SHOES

22 🔂 MAP P66, C3

The shoes at Pisaverde are quite a sight, with each pair uniquely fashioned and handcrafted with bold and brightly coloured leather and all manner of fabrics (including recycled materials too, such as car tyres). If you want some unique shoes to strut on the street, this is the place. Check out the full-length boot made for a drag queen. (☎922 31 41 28; www.pisaverdestore.com; Calle Juan de Vera 7; ☻10am-8.30pm Mon-Fri, 11am-2.30pm Sat)

Atelier & Co   VINTAGE

Stuffed with browse-worthy goodies, this shop (see **22** 🔂 Map p66, C3), has an excellent range of vintage clothing, as well as jewellery, wine,

collectables, bric-a-brac and odds and ends. (☎669 43 39 92; Calle Capitán Brotóns 6; ☻10am-2pm & 5-8.30pm Mon-Fri, 10am-2pm Sat)

Jumping Man   MUSIC

Owned by music buff Fernando, Jumping Man (see **22** 🔂 Map p66, C3) has a petite space stuffed with jazz, soul, funk, R & B, hip-hop, pop and rock vinyl and CDs, much of it classic material from the 1960s through to the noughties. There's always something good playing too; once you start browsing, it's hard to stop. (Calle Bencomo 30; ☻10am-2pm & 5-9pm Mon-Fri, 10am-2pm Sat)

ADC Diseño del Siglo   DESIGN

23 🔂 MAP P66, B3

You may not want to stuff a 1950s lampshade or a 1960s injection-moulded swivel armchair into your luggage, but the funktastic 20th-century vintage pieces on display at this small gallery deliver an eye-catching survey of some of the most iconic design trends from the last 100 years. (www.adcvintage.com; Calle Ascanio y Nieves 1; ☻10am-1pm & 5.30-8.30pm Tue-Fri, 10.30am-1.30pm Sat)

El Rincon Extremeño   FOOD

24 🔂 MAP P66, B3

A good place to buy *jamón ibérico de bellota* (from acorn-fed black pigs), priced at around €40 a kilo. Other less costly hams are available – a whole leg or, if this is a worrying protuberance from your

A Brief History of Tenerife

The Guanches
The first people to live here were the aboriginal Guanches, who were persecuted and driven out by waves of marauding invaders. Thought to be related to the Berbers of North Africa, how the Guanches arrived here is a mystery as they apparently possessed no boats.

Conquests & Affluence
The first major conquest of the island was by French adventurer Jean de Béthencourt in the 15th century. He was backed by the Spanish Catholic monarchs who had already taken Granada on the mainland. With the discovery of the New World, Tenerife became a wealthy trading post, first for sugar and subsequently grapes, which were used for producing Malmsey wine, then considered to be the best in the world. This wealthy period of history is reflected in the grandiose colonial-style buildings in La Laguna and La Orotava. Spain's control of the islands didn't go unchallenged. The most spectacular success went to Admiral Robert Blake, under Cromwell, who annihilated a Spanish treasure fleet at Santa Cruz. British harassment culminated in 1797 with Admiral Nelson's attack on the city, when he not only failed to storm the town but lost his right arm in the fighting.

Economic Woes
The Canaries were declared a province of Spain in 1821 and Santa Cruz de Tenerife was made the capital. The economic fallout from the Spanish Civil War and World War II plunged the islands into economic misery. Many Canarios opted to emigrate, including 16,000 who headed for Venezuela, one third of whom perished in the ocean crossings.

The Onset of Tourism
Not until the 1960s did the economy start to pick up with the onset of tourism to the islands, particularly from the UK and Germany. In 1978 Tenerife opened the Reina Sofía airport in the south, which concurrently led to the mass development of the Playa de las Américas. Today the majority of tourists head for the southern resorts, although the numbers are gradually shifting as more visitors discover the quieter, greener and more traditional side of the island in the interior and the north.

Catedral (p67)

hand luggage, sliced and shrink-wrapped. You can enjoy a taster (€1.80 to €4), including cheese such as the prize-winning Majorero from Fuerteventura. (📞922 26 65 08; www.elrinconextremeno.net; Plaza Concepción 1; ⏰9am-11pm Mon-Sat, to 3pm Sun)

Atlantida Artesania   FOOD & DRINK

25 🔒 MAP P66, C3

Jam-packed with preserves, pickles, *gofio* (ground, roasted grain), *mojo*, cheeses, honey, local wines and cigars, this corner *vinoteca* also stocks Tierra de Perros, a locally brewed organic beer. It offers tastings of Canarian wine to encourage

your browsing (and buying!), as well as serving tapas (📞922 25 22 92; Calle San Agustín 55; ⏰9.30am-1pm & 5-8.30pm Mon-Fri, 10am-2pm Sun)

Dicky Morgan   VINTAGE

26 🔒 MAP P66, B3

Look for the blue-on-blue exterior of this fabulous vintage shop. Dicky Morgan's edgy take on fashion, furniture and art is coupled with a big-city outlook and a fun sense of humour – check out the awesome 1950s shades and terrific hand-bags. (📞922 26 70 64; www.facebook.com/dickymorgantf; Calle San Agustín 75; ⏰10.30am-8.30pm Mon-Sat, to 2pm Sun)

Explore ◈

Puerto de la Cruz

Scenically spread over the slopes of north Tenerife, Puerto de la Cruz is the elder statesman of Tenerife tourism. Its history of welcoming foreign visitors dates back to the late 19th century, and these days the easy-going town is a charming destination with genuine character. There are stylish boardwalks, beaches with safe swimming, traditional restaurants, and lots of pretty parks and churches.

The Short List

○ **Jardín Botánico (p78)** Smelling the flowers at this marvellous botanical garden filled with winding pathways.

○ **Risco Belle Aquatic Gardens (p84)** Relaxing in the presence of herons and dragonflies or grabbing a coffee on the lawns.

○ **Playa Martiánez (p85)** Sunbathing on the black, volcanic sand or learning to surf in gentle waves.

○ **Tito's Bodeguita (p87)** Tucking into island specialities and washing it all down with a little local wine.

○ **Ebano Café (p88)** Watching the locals walk by as you sip on a cool cocktail or a cup of coffee.

Getting There & Around

🚌 The long-distance buses starting in or passing through Puerto de la Cruz often double up as local buses. Buses arrive at Calle Hermanos Fernández Perdigón. Bus 103 is a direct service from Santa Cruz (€5.25, 55 minutes).

🚗 Taxis are widely available and relatively inexpensive (a 15-minute ride should cost around €5).

Puerto de la Cruz Map on p82

La Ranilla (p81) FRITZ16/SHUTTERSTOCK ©

Top Experience
Jardín Botánico

Puerto de la Cruz is home to several magnificent parks; the crowning glory is the Jardín Botánico, a lush subtropical garden primarily dedicated to Canarian flora, with more than 30,000 specimens over 2.5 hectares. It's a peaceful haven, with plenty of birdsong, fragrant flowers and a meandering pathway that takes you on a fascinating botanical journey around the globe.

◎ MAP P82, H5

☏ 922 92 29 81

Calle Retama 2

adult/child €3/free

🕑 9am-6pm;

🅿

Explore the History

Ask for the free brochure, which relates the fascinating background of the gardens. They were created by the Royal Order of Carlos III in 1788 as a staging post for cultivating plant and tree species imported from the tropics, with the eventual plan to introduce them to the royal gardens in Madrid. Unsurprisingly, the Spanish mainland proved too cool, so this second phase wilted away.

Extraordinary Trees

These gardens are a lost world of fairy-tale trees, including the 200-year-old massive Australian Moreton bay fig, with its wall-like buttress roots; the reptilian monkey puzzle tree from the Andes; South American silk floss with bizarre spiky trunks of armour; and several varieties of palms, including the skyscraper Phoenix *canariensis*.

The Lily Pond

This is the perfect shady place to relax on a warm summer's day. And what better place to grab some bench time than overlooking a dreamy lily pond with sunbasking terrapins and darting dragonflies, against a subtropical backdrop of plants and trees? It's a world away from the clamour of the coast.

Nearby: Risco Belle Aquatic Gardens

Less than 1km west of Jardín Botánico, in Parque Taoro, the Risco Belle Aquatic Gardens (p84) resemble a Renoir canvas, with a sweeping lawn frontage studded with citrus trees, water features and tropical plants, as well as cafe tables and chairs. From here, hidden paths lead to a lily-filled lake with waterfalls and bridges where swooping herons and leisurely waterfowl add to the painterly setting.

★ Top Tips

o Try to reschedule your visit if you spy a tour bus outside; it can get crowded.

o Take water (and snacks for any children); no refreshments are available on-site.

o Pathways may be wet; wear sensible footwear.

o It's quite a long walk from the centre; several buses stop at the gardens en route out of town. Check www.titsa.com for a timetable.

✕ Take a Break

o There is a pizzeria plus several other restaurants directly facing the front entrance to the Jardín Botánico on Calle Retama.

o The nearby Hotel Botánico has a few excellent restaurants, including **La Parrilla** (☏ 922 38 14 00; www.hotelbotanico. com; Avenida Richard J Yeoward 1; mains €10-16; ⏰ 6.30am-10.30pm Sat-Wed; 🛜), specialising in upmarket Spanish cuisine.

Walking Tour 🥾

A Fishy Trail

This charming multifaceted resort town has its roots firmly in the seafaring and fishing industries. While the small harbour is physically and culturally still at the heart of Puerto de la Cruz, the surrounding tangled net of streets is one of the most fashionable parts of Puerto for locals-in-the-know, with its terraced bars and scenic squares.

Walk Facts

Start Churreria Perdomo
End Calle Mequínez
Length 1km; 1½ hours

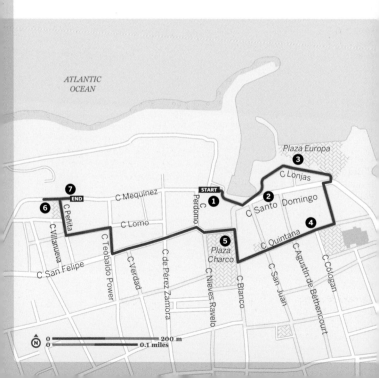

❶ Harbour Churros

For the best churros in town, join the local fisherfolk at harbour-front **Churrería Perdomo** (churros €1; ⏱6am-6pm Mon-Sat) for a portion of these hot and crispy spiral-shaped doughnuts dunked into hot chocolate. This hole-in-the-wall spot, with a Virgin above the door, sells *porras* as well – larger tubular doughnuts, also quick fried and utterly irresistible.

❷ Calle Santo Domingo

This shopping street has a couple of gems on it, including **Rhodian House** (p92), selling jewellery made from natural abalone, mother of pearl and seashells, and **Marysol** (p92), one of the first shops to open here back in the '80s, specialising in fine jewellery, with some Guanche motifs included in the designs.

❸ Fresh-off-the-Boat Seafood

Owned by the local fisherfolk, **La Cofradía de Pescadores** (p88) is quite simply the best place for eating seafood in town – unless you buy it fresh from the fish stall next door to cook yourself! The back terrace has appropriate fishing-harbour views.

❹ Terraza Time

Fronting the same-named hotel, **Terraza Marquesa** (p89), dating from 1712, has one of the most delightful terraces to sip a drink and people-watch. It overlooks the lovely 16th-century Iglesia de San Francisco and adjacent flower-filled plaza, and there's live traditional Canarian music here nightly from 7pm to 11pm.

❺ Pause in the Plaza

The fantastic central square of **Plaza Charco** (p84; the name translates as 'Puddle Plaza' – it used to flood from the sea every time it was stormy) is shaded by trees and palms. It's the town's meeting spot, with kiosks, benches and a children's playground. It's surrounded by bars and restaurants.

❻ La Ranilla

Continue to this pretty plaza in La Ranilla *barrio* (district) where brightly coloured fisherfolk's cottages have been transformed into fashionable restaurants and bars, including **Agora** (p89), a casual, popular cafe and cocktail bar with art exhibitions, books visitors can borrow and magazines to read. Tables overlook one of the prettiest squares in town.

❼ Calle Mequínez

Nip around the corner to this lively street, home to a handful of chilled-out places to eat and drink, including **Bodega Julian** (p87), with its reassuringly brief menu of specialities like cod on sweet potato and succulent roasted lamb. The owners are accomplished musicians so live music is an added plus.

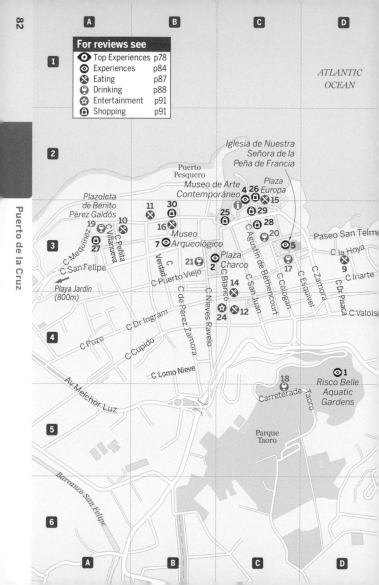

For reviews see

- ⦿ Top Experiences p78
- ◉ Experiences p84
- ✖ Eating p87
- ⬤ Drinking p88
- ✪ Entertainment p91
- 🔒 Shopping p91

ATLANTIC OCEAN

Iglesia de Nuestra Señora de la Peña de Francia

Puerto Pesquero

Museo de Arte Contemporáneo

Plaza Europa

Plazoleta de Benito Pérez Galdós

Museo Arqueológico

Plaza Charco

Paseo San Telm

C la Hoya

C Iriarte

C Dr Pisaca

C Valois

Playa Jardín (800m)

C San Felipe

C Mequinez

C Peñita

C Vilanueva

C Puerto Viejo

C de Pérez Zamora

C Nieves Ravelo

C Blanco

C San Juan

C Agustín de Béthencourt

C Colgán

C Esquivel

C Zamora

C Verdad

C Dr Ingram

C Pozo

C Cupido

C Lomo Nieve

Av Melchor Luz

Barranco San Felipe

Carretera de Taoro

Risco Belle Aquatic Gardens

Parque Taoro

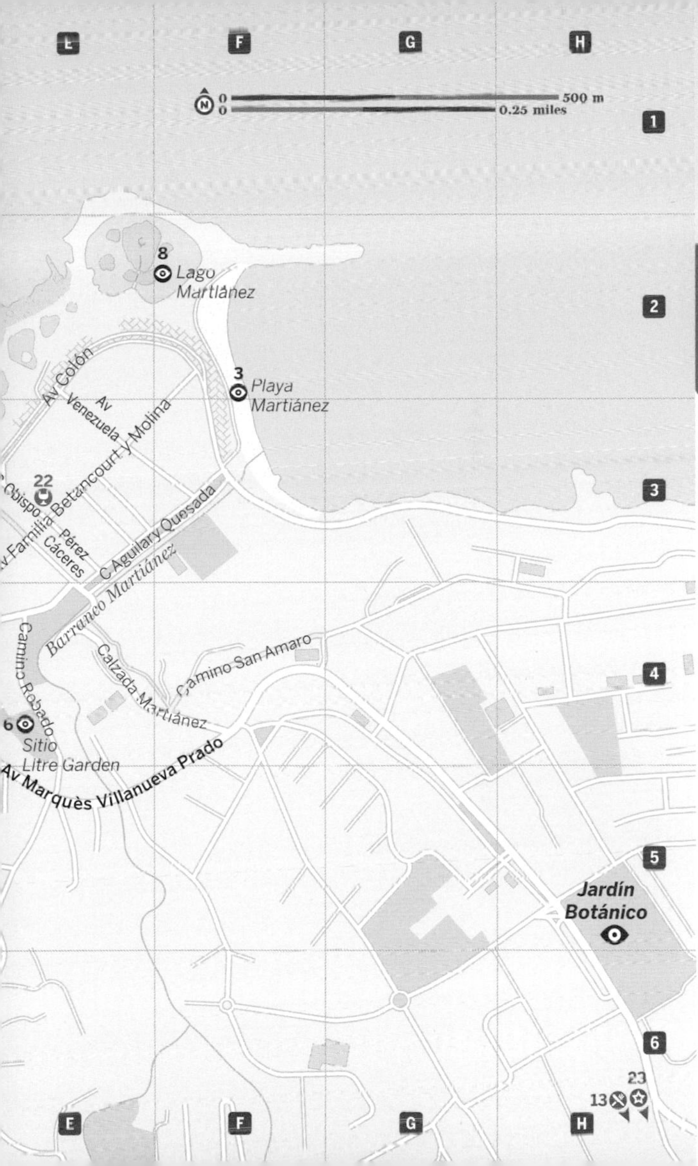

E **F** **G** **H**

1

Ⓝ 0 ——————————— 500 m
0 ——————————— 0.25 miles

2

8 ⊙ *Lago Martiánez*

Av Colón

Av Venezuela

3 ⊙ *Playa Martiánez*

3

22 ⊙

C Obispita
Av Familia Betancourt y Molina
Pérez Cáceres
C Aguilar y Quesada

Barranco Martiánez

Camino Rabado
Calzada Martiánez
Camino San Amaro

4

6 ⊙
Sitio Litre Garden

Av Marquès Villanueva Prado

5

Jardín Botánico ⊙

6

23 ☆
13 ✕
▼ ▼

E **F** **G** **H**

Experiences

Risco Belle Aquatic Gardens

GARDENS

1 👁 MAP P82, D4

This is not just any old garden: step through the entrance and you'll be met by a sweeping lawn punctuated with tables and chairs, tropical plants (birds of paradise and poinsettias) and citrus trees. In the historic main house there's a cafe serving drinks and snacks.

For a small admission fee you can also visit the magnificent aquatic gardens with herons, dragonflies, a mock lookout tower and benches for quiet contemplation.

With a backdrop of green and birdsong, these gardens feel a world away from the clamour of the coast. Don't miss them. (Parque Taoro; adult/child €4/free; 🕙9.30am-6pm; 🅿)

Plaza Charco

SQUARE

2 👁 MAP P82, B3

The magnificent central square of Plaza Charco (the names translates as 'Puddle Plaza' – it used to flood from the sea every time it was stormy) is shaded by Indian laurel trees and Canary palms. It's the town's meeting-and-greeting place, with kiosks, benches and a children's play-ground, and is flanked by relaxing bars and restaurants.

Playa Martiánez

Playa Martíanez

BEACH

3 ◎ MAP P82, F2

The long and sandy Playa Martiánez is at the eastern end of town, where a large jetty filters the anger of Atlantic swells and turns them into mere gentle rollers, perfect for learning to surf on. As with other beaches in town, the sand is black and volcanic, consisting of small particles of basalt. (Avenida Colón)

Museo de Arte Contemporáneo

GALLERY

4 ◎ MAP P82, C2

The first contemporary-art museum to open in Spain, dating from 1953, this well-displayed collection includes outstanding foreign, Spanish and Canarian artists such as Will Faber, Óscar Domínguez and César Manrique. The setting, in the historic former customs house, is almost as inspiring as the artwork. (Casa de la Aduana, Calle Lonjas; adult/child €1.50/free; ⏰10am-2pm Mon-Sat)

Iglesia de Nuestra Señora de la Peña de Francia

CHURCH

5 ◎ MAP P82, C3

This pretty 17th-century church boasts three naves, a wooden Mudéjar ceiling and a carved wood effigy of Gran Poder de Dios, one of the town's most revered saints, carved in around 1706. Side chapels include one dedicated to the Virgen del Carmen. The church is fronted by lush and attractive land-

Beach Life

☀

Puerto de la Cruz is home to several beaches, largely sheltered from waves and perfect for young children, though breakers can be found for surfing. In the heart of the town are the rocky and attractive coves around the little port just below the Paseo San Telmo, while the main beaches are Playa Martiánez and **Playa Jardín** (Paseo Luis Lavagi; Ⓟ).

scaped gardens, decorated with flowers, palms and *drago* (dragon) trees. (Calle Quintana; ⏰8am-6pm)

Sitio Litre Garden

GARDENS

6 ◎ MAP P82, E4

This delightful garden is exquisitely laid out with walkways, fountains, tropical and subtropical plants and flowers, plus the oldest *drago* tree in town. The highlight is the orchid walk through the greenhouse, with its well-displayed and signed orchids. There's an inviting terrace cafe and a (surprisingly tacky) gift shop. The gardens have an interesting British history, which you can read about in the free leaflet.

Take note of the croquet lawn, with everything in place ready for a game. Well, aside from the cucumber sandwiches, that is... (www.jardindeorquideas.com; Camino Robado; adult/child €4.75/free; ⏰9.30am-5pm)

Foodie Heaven

Dining is one of the undeniable highlights here as Puerto de la Cruz is a serious foodie destination. Peruse the former fishers' quarter of La Ranilla, just a couple of streets north of Plaza Charco, for a large choice of the town's most innovative restaurants. Names come and go in the shifting culinary sands of Puerto de la Cruz, but there's nonetheless a solid bedrock of established eateries.

TF-5; Tito's is located just beyond exit 35. Alternatively, hop in a taxi (approximately €7 from the town centre). (922 08 94 36; www.titosbodeguita.com; Camino de Duraznol; mains €10-16; 12.30-11pm Mon-Sat)

Tasca el Olivo   MEDITERRANEAN €€

14 MAP P82, C4

The Mediterranean cuisine here is soundly prepared and spiked with a soupçon or two of innovation. Surf-and-turf choices such as pork loins with prawns, and wholesome servings of chickpeas with chorizo, ribs and bacon or assorted smoked fish have won the restaurant a local fan base. (922 38 01 17; www.tascaelolivo. eatbu.com; Calle Iriarte 1; mains €9-15; 1-10pm Wed & Thu, 1-10.30pm Fri & Sat, 1-4pm Sun)

La Cofradía de Pescadores   SEAFOOD €€

15 MAP P82, C2

Come here for the catch of the day. Watch the cost though, as some fish dishes are priced per weight. The back terrace allows you look out on the fishing harbour. Alternatively, buy it at the fish stall next door and cook it yourself. (922 38 34 09; Calle Lonjas 5; mains €12-20; noon-3pm)

Restaurante Mil Sabores   MEDITERRANEAN €€

16 MAP P82, B3

Styling itself as a temple to modern Mediterranean cooking, this flash, blue-fronted restaurant has the looks and the tastes down to a fine art. Expect dishes like homemade quiche with roasted vegetables, avocado with tiger prawns or Iberian ham croquettes, and a perfectly combined mix of pork, apple and bacon. It's quite dressy, without being formal. Reservations recommended. (922 36 81 72; Calle Cruz Verde 5; mains €9-16; noon-11pm Fri-Wed)

Drinking

Ebano Café   CAFE

17 MAP P82, C3

This cafe is located in a beautiful building seasoned with an age-old patina and with plenty of original features. It's equally ideal for sipping a cocktail or surfing the web with a decent cappuccino. Sit outside in one of the comfy wicker chairs (they get taken quickly so you may need to move fast), within confessional distance of the church. Tapas are also served. (☎ 922 38 86 32; Calle la Hoya 2; ⏰ 9am-11.30pm; 🛜)

Terraza Taoro
BAR

18 🚌 MAP P82, C5

Once you've clambered up the 200-odd steps to get here from the centre of town, you deserve a long cool drink as well as some supreme panoramic views of the town and coast from the sweeping terrace. Speciality coffees and fancy cocktails are justifiably popular; sweet and savoury snacks are also available. (☎ 922 38 88 68; www. terrazataoro.es/es; Carretera de Taoro 9; ⏰ 10am-10pm Sun-Thu, to 11pm Fri & Sat)

Agora
COCKTAIL BAR

19 🚌 MAP P82, A3

This relaxed, popular cocktail bar and cafe allows you to take in art exhibits and peruse books and magazines while looking out onto one of the most picturesque squares in the area. It's a lovely spot for a dose of early morning sun while relaxing in a bamboo chair out front. To eat there are tapas, and come evening the cocktails start from €4. (Plazoleta de Benito Pérez Galdós 6; ⏰ 10am-12.30am Tue-Sun, 3-11pm Mon; 🛜)

Terraza Marquesa
BAR

20 🚌 MAP P82, C3

Fronting the same-named hotel, Terraza Marquesa, dating from 1712, has one of the most delightful terraces to sip a drink and people-watch. It overlooks the lovely 16th-century Iglesia de San Francisco and adjacent flower-filled plaza, and there's live traditional Canarian music here nightly from 7pm to 11pm. (☎ 922 38 31 51; www. hotelmarquesa.com; Calle Quintana 11; ⏰ 8am-2am)

Restaurante Cafetería Dinámico
BAR

Bars and cafes come and go in Puerto de la Cruz but the Dinámico (see 2 ◉ Map p82, B3) has been around since the '50s in one form or another and has counted the Beatles and Agatha Christie among former patrons. It's a sprawling terraced place in the centre of Plaza Charco with a Latin American vibe and more character than most others spots around the square. (Plaza Charco; ⏰ 7am-12.30am Sun-Thu, to 2am Fri & Sat; 🛜)

Colours Café
COCKTAIL BAR

21 🚌 MAP P82, B3

Above a pizzeria on an energetic stretch of eateries along the western flank of Plaza Charco, this cocktail bar is the perfect spot to snag a window seat overlooking the square. With mellow decor

Arts & Culture

Architecture

There is really no such thing as typical Canarian architecture, as there have been so many different influences over the centuries and it is not uncommon for a building to reflect more than one architecture style. The colonial period is a good example of this architectural potpourri, typically reflecting elements from the Spanish, Portuguese, French, Italian and English architectural schools. Baroque influences are also in evidence, in particular in the beautiful carved wooden balconies and internal courtyards in the historic centres of La Orotava and La Laguna. Fast-forward to the present and the late great César Manrique, whose ecologically sensitive creations are visible throughout the islands, including Tenerife.

Painting

Tenerife's earliest-known art forms date back to the cave paintings of the Guanches. The best-loved sculpture from these times is the *Ídolo de tara*, a curvy feminine figure and Guanche idol, which you can see stamped on souvenir T-shirts and pottery. Among the best-known Tenerife artists is 17th-century Gaspar de Quevedo, impressionist Manuel González (1843–1909) and the famous local exponent of surrealism, Óscar Domínguez (1906–57), whose work you can see at several museums here including the Tenerife Espacio de las Artes (TEA) in Santa Cruz.

Crafts

Fine lacework and embroidered tablecloths, napkins and table linen can be found throughout the island and, although admittedly dated, they are exquisite, reflecting skills that have been handed down through generations. Beware of cheap Chinese imports (easily identifiable as they are far cheaper). Other popular items to weigh down your hand luggage include handwoven baskets, carpets and rugs.

Music

The symbol of the Canarios' musical heritage is the *timple*, a ukulele-style instrument of obscure origin, thought to have been introduced to the islands by Berber slaves in the 15th century. It's a small wooden, five-stringed instrument, which you will always see being played at traditional fiestas for dances such as the *isa* and *folía* and, if you're lucky, the *tajareste*, the only known dance to be passed down by the ancient Guanches.

and Latin and African music, it's a good place to kick off your night on the tiles with an El Diablo or a Tequilla Sour. Cocktails are €5.50. (Plaza Charco; 8pm-2am Wed-Mon)

Azucar

CLUB

22 MAP P82, E3

This dark and sexy Latino nightclub goes on all night and is located in an atmospheric colonial building. (682 28 67 05; www.facebook.com/DiscotecaAzucar Tenerife; Calle Obispo Pérez Cáceres; 10.30pm-6am)

Entertainment

Abaco

CONCERT VENUE

23 MAP P82, H6

This sumptuous historical mansion, about 1.5km southeast of the town centre, hosts classical-music concerts on Sunday evenings and traditional Canarian folklore concerts on Wednesdays. The interior, with its period furniture, original artwork and ornate finishes, is a delight. There's also an inviting Sky Sports–free bar, although a round of drinks will cost a lot more than the round-trip taxi ride back to town.

The house museum (€10) can be explored with a guide between 10am and 1.30pm every day except Tuesday and Sunday. (922 37 01 07; www.abacotenerife.com; Casa Grande, El Durazno; 1-4pm & 6.30-11pm)

A History of Tourism

Until it was declared an independent town in the early 20th century, Puerto de la Cruz was merely the port of the wealthier area of La Orotava. Bananas, wine, sugar and cochineal (dye-producing insects) were exported from here, and a substantial bourgeois class developed in the 1700s. In the 1800s the English arrived, first as merchants and later as sun-seeking holidaymakers, marking the beginning of the tourist transformation that characterises the town today.

Blanco Bar

LIVE MUSIC

24 MAP P82, C4

As well as live music, there are also comedy acts here, which may not tickle your funny bone unless you speak Spanish (check what's on via the website beforehand). It has a great atmosphere, with inexpensive drinks and free entry to many (but not all) concerts. It also hosts art exhibitions. (620 955197; www.blancobar.com; Calle Blanco 12; 8pm-3am Sun-Thu, 9pm-5.30am Fri & Sat;)

Shopping

Jamónes Riviera

FOOD

25 MAP P82, C3

This market-style stall is a daily institution, and where locals come to stock up on all those deli goodies, including cheese, chorizo and the famous *jamón serrano* (Serrano ham), which can be sold vacuum-packed if you're looking for a particularly salivatory souvenir to impress the folks back home. (harbour; ⊙9am-10pm)

Casa de la Aduana   ARTS & CRAFTS

26 🔒 MAP P82, C2

You'll find the most comprehensive selection of quality crafts in town here. It's not cheap but there's no souvenir tat; expect to discover classy locally produced jewellery, finely crafted ceramics, stoneware and glassware, quirky children's toys, elegant hand-painted fans and tasteful textiles (with not one *I Love Tenerife* T-shirt in sight). The adjacent delicatessen and bodega specialises in local wines and gourmet products. (📞922 37 81 03; Calle Lonjas 8-10; ⊙10am-8pm Mon-Sat)

La Ranilla   ARTS & CRAFTS

27 🔒 MAP P82, A3

Look for a tiny former fisherman's cottage painted brilliant turquoise; it's now the happy home to this crafts shop specialising in innovative local handmade art and handicrafts, including jewellery, ceramics, textiles and toys. No straw donkeys here. (📞922 38 50 87; Calle Mequínez 59; ⊙10am-2pm & 5-8pm Mon-Fri, 10am-2pm Sat)

Marysol   JEWELLERY

28 🔒 MAP P82, C3

Swiss-owned Marysol was one of the first shops to open back in the '80s and specialises in fine jewellery made with coral, lava, silver, steel and olivine, with some Guanche motifs included in the designs. (Calle Santo Domingo 6; ⊙10am-8pm Mon-Sat)

Rhodian House   JEWELLERY

29 🔒 MAP P82, C3

The shopping street of Calle Santo Domingo has a couple of gems on it, including Rhodian House, which

Quirky Festivals

Aside from a riotous Carnaval celebration, Puerto has some other fun-filled, and thoroughly weird, fiestas:

San Juan Held on the eve of the saint's day (23 June). Bonfires light the sky and, in a throwback to Guanche times, goats (and other animals) are dragged to the sea off Playa Jardín for a ritual bathing, in a practice that some visitors may find objectionable.

Fiesta de los Cacharros This is a quaint festival where children rush through the streets, dragging behind them a string of old pots, kettles, pans, car spares, tin cans – just about anything that will make a racket, all in honour of San Andrés (St Andrew). It's held on 29 November.

Dragon Trees: A Long, Shady Past

Among the more curious trees you will see in Tenerife is the *drago* (dragon tree; *Dracaena draco*), which can reach a height of 18m and live for centuries.

Having survived the last ice age, the tree looks prehistoric, unusual and unique. Its shape resembles a giant posy of flowers, its trunk and branches being the stems, which break into bunches of long, narrow, silvery-green leaves higher up. As the plant (technically it is not a tree, though it's always referred to as one) grows, it becomes more and more top-heavy. To stabilise itself, the *drago* ingeniously grows roots on the outside of its trunk, eventually creating a second wider trunk. What makes the *drago* stranger still is its red sap or resin – known, of course, as 'dragon's blood' – which was traditionally used in medicine.

The plant once played an important role in Canary Island life, for it was beneath the ancient branches of a *drago* that the Guanche Council of Nobles would gather to administer justice.

The *drago* is one of a family of up to 40 species *(Dracaena)* that survived the ice age in tropical and subtropical zones of the Old World, and is one of the last representatives of Tertiary-era flora.

sells jewellery primarily made from natural abalone, mother of pearl and colourful seashells. (Calle Santo Domingo 4; ◷10am-1.30pm & 4-8pm Mon-Fri, to 1.30pm Sat)

Licoreria Puerto
FOOD & DRINKS

This is the place (see 9 ✕ Map p82, D3) to stock up on some edible mementos from a wide array of Canarian specialities, including banana wine (available for tasting), *mojo* spices, aloe-vera products and ecological preserves, honey, cactus marmalade and

sweets. (☎922 38 18 15; Calle la Hoya 22; ◷10am-8pm Mon-Sat)

Carey
FASHION & ACCESSORIES

30 🔒 MAP P82, B3

An enchanting small boutique selling beautifully crafted jewellery, designer-look women's fashion and casual-chic accessories, including sequined belts and glittery evening bags. (☎922 38 87 23; Calle Mequínez 13; ◷11am-2pm & 4-7pm Mon-Thu, 11am-2pm & 5-8pm Fri, 10.30am-1.30pm Sat)

Explore 🏛️

La Orotava

This colonial town has the lot, it seems: cobblestone streets, flower-filled plazas and more Castilian mansions than the rest of the island put together. Along with La Laguna, La Orotava is one of the loveliest towns on Tenerife, and one of the most truly 'Canarian' places in the Canary Islands.

The Short List

○ **Casa de los Balcones (p96)** *Photographing the traditional balconies adorning this elaborate 17th-century mansion.*

○ **Jardines del Marquesado de la Quinta Roja (p101)** *Taking a wander through carefully landscaped gardens.*

○ **Iglesia de la Concepción (p101)** *Gazing at the elaborate interior of this beautiful baroque church.*

○ **Bar la Duquesa (p103)** *Lunching on hearty Canarian food in a family-run setting.*

○ **Canarias Concept (p106)** *Shopping for authentic locally-made crafts and cuisine.*

Getting There & Around

🚗 Parking in La Orotava is a nightmare.

🚌 From Puerto de la Cruz, it is 9km. Bus 345 from Puerto de la Cruz (€1.45, 20 minutes) leaves roughly every half hour from 5.55am to 10.10pm.

🚶 You could arrive on foot from Puerto de la Cruz – it takes around an hour. The town centre is easily navigable on foot.,

La Orotava Map on p100

Jardines del Marquesado de la Quinta Roja (p101)

Top Experience
Casa de los Balcones

Calle San Francisco is home to La Orotava's highest concentration of 17th-century architectural gems, dating from the time when the town was home to Tenerife's wealthiest aristocrats. Arguably the most good-looking of the traditional balconied mansions here is the justifiably popular Casa de los Balcones, dating to 1632, with its balconies arranged around a picturesque central courtyard as well as decorating the front of the building.

◉ MAP P100, A5

www.casa-balcones.com

Casa Fonesca, Calle San Francisco 3

courtyard & museum €5

⏱ 8.30am-6.30pm

Culture & Crafts

Ground-floor rooms are set around a leafy central patio packed with memorabilia. One room is devoted to lacework, where you can admire the fine local needlework; there may be a demonstration too. There's also a traditional bodega where you can ask for a taste of the banana liquor.

Museum

Many tourists don't stray further than the ground-floor exhibition and sales space, missing out on the delightfully quirky 1st-floor museum. Rooms are furnished with 17th-century antiques; the granny in bed will make you smile. This is also the best place for photographing the building, with fabulous views of the courtyard below with its intricate woodwork carving.

Nearby: Casa Lercaro

This 16th-century mansion (p102) is widely considered to be the most representative building constructed in traditional Canary Island style. Particularly noteworthy is the finely carved baroque decoration on the woodwork, including the magnificent traditional balconies. The interior plant-filled courtyard is now a restaurant; look for the 17th-century sculpture entitled **Adoración de los pastores** from the Genoa school. Part of the building also houses a decor shop.

★ Top Tips

o This sight is very popular with tour groups, so if possible try to visit early in the morning or in the late afternoon.

o Parking nearby is difficult and restricted, so come by bus or taxi if you can.

o Drop by the tourist office to pick up a map of other grand historic mansions around La Orotava, many of which are near Casa de los Balcones.

✕ Take a Break

o Grab a table on the cobble road and enjoy a midmorning tapa at the decent local Bar la Duquesa (p103).

o Otherwise, swoon at the amazing valley views from Tascafe Grimaldi (p105) in Casa Lercaro and have a drink or something more filling.

Walking Tour 🚶

Timeless Tascas & Crafts

Tucked in between leafy courtyards and steep winding streets are shops selling beautifully made local crafts and gourmet items, while cultural history is kept alive via still-functioning mills. And if you hear that distinctive slap of dominoes, follow the sound, as it will doubtless take you to one of the town's numerous old-fashioned tascas (bars); great for inexpensive tapas – and atmosphere.

Walk Facts

Start Café los Balcones
End MAIT
Length 0.8km; one hour

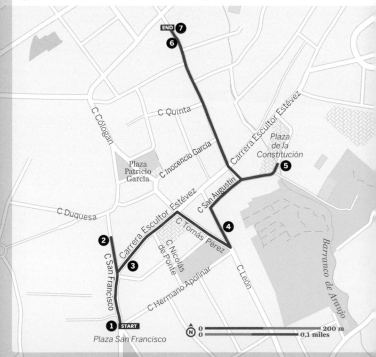

❶ Café los Balcones

Bypassed by tourists marching to the centre of town, the **Café los Balcones** (Calle San Francisco 10; breakfast €3-5; ⏱8am-7.30pm Mon-Fri, 9.30am-5pm Sat) is a no-frills cafe-cum-*tasca* set in a historic building and a great place to kick-start your day with excellent coffee along with a *tostada con tomate* (toast topped with tomatoes and olive oil). Omelettes and such are also available.

❷ La Maquina, Molino de Gofio

Gofio is basically milled wheat and corn with the consistency of wholegrain flour. It was once the staple diet of the Guanches. At **La Maquina** (p102) you can watch the miller at work grinding the grain, and buy a small bag of *gofio*, which can be sprinkled on cereal or desserts or eaten with warm milk.

❸ Canarian Handicrafts

As the name implies, **Canarias Concept** (p106) sells just Canarian-made crafts and products. It has a large showroom packed with jewellery, ceramics, artwork, handmade toys, ornaments, glazed tiles, soap, scarves and T-shirts, plus a gourmet section and local wines.

❹ Torta Time

Founded in 1916, **Casa Egon** (p104) is the oldest *pasteleria* (cake shop) in the Canaries and has happily maintained its stuck-in-a-time-warp ambience with custard-coloured paintwork, antique weighing scales, original floor tiles and woodwork. The cakes include all-time local favourites such as *anis*-based *roscos* and apple-filled *cabello de angel*. There's a simple, traditional restaurant out back.

❺ Liceo de Taoro

The 19th-century **Liceo de Taoro** (p106) has a magnificent setting high above the square. It's now a private club, where you can still order a drink from the bar within and take it to the front terrace that overlooks the ornamental gardens and the rooftops beyond.

❻ Casa Torrehermosa

Tenerife's excellent art-and-crafts chain Artenerife has its local outlet in this magnificent 17th-century mansion. **Casa Torrehermosa** (p106) provides a fitting setting for the display of locally produced artwork, pottery, jewellery and crafts. Maps, posters and cards are also available.

❼ MAIT

Situated inside a former 17th-century convent, this **shop** (p106) sells an excellent selection of Ibero-American art and crafts. You'll find everything from ornaments, T-shirts and knitwear right through to nativity figures, woven rugs and baskets, toys and jewellery. It's all displayed beautifully in a spacious and well-organised showroom.

La Orotava

For reviews see

- ⊙ Top Experiences p96
- ⊙ Experiences p101
- ✗ Eating p103
- 🍷 Drinking p106
- 🔒 Shopping p106

C Calvario

C Tejar

Plaza Franchi Alfaro

Plaza San Sebastián

Av Obispo Benítez

C García Beltrán

C Calvario

C de Juan Cullén

Av Luque Moreno

Museo de Artesanía Iberoamericana

⊙3 C Santo Domingo

C Nicandro González Borges

C Juan Padrón

21 🔒20
🔒 Av de Canarias
✗12 Av Sor Soledad Cobiá

C Camino de Lugo

Parque Nacional del Teide Administrative Offices

19 🔒

C Viera

C Tomás Zerolo

C Rosales

C N'candro González Borges

C Cantos Canarios

Iglesia de San Agustín

C Gral Caraveo Grimaldi

C Cólogan

C Magistrado Barreda

C Quinta

C Balcón

C Silla

C Inocencio García

Carrera Escultor Estévez

Plaza de la Constitución

⊙17

C Educadora Lucía Mesa

9 ✗

C Colegio

Plaza Patricio García

⊙2 Iglesia de la Concepción

10 ✗

C Tomás Pérez

C San Augustín

✗11

⊙1 Jardines del Marquesado de la Quinta Roja

C Duquesa

Casa Lercaro

4 ⊙
⊙14

C Colegio

La Maquina

6 ⊙

16 ✗

18 ✗

C Nicolás Ponte R

C Linares

Hijuela del Botánico

8 ⊙

C Hermano Apolinar

C León

Av Carrero Blanco

Casa de los Balcones

⊙ Radapalla

13 ✗

C San Francisco

5 ⊙ ✗7

Casa del Turista

Museo de las Alfombras

C San Juan

C Altavista

Plaza San Francisco

C Cantillo

Plaza San Juan

C Fernando Fuentes

C Dr Domingo González García

C Nueva

C Bicha

C San Juan

C Romulo Betancourt

N 0 _____ 200 m
   0 _____ 0.1 miles

15 ✗

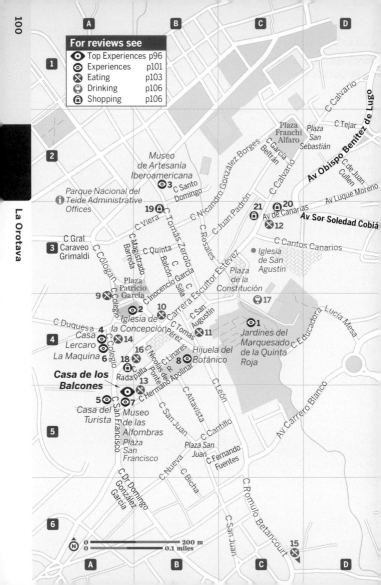

Experiences

Jardínes del Marquesado de la Quinta Roja
GARDENS

1 MAP P100, C4

Also known as the Jardín Victoria, these French-influenced 18th-century gardens cascade in terraces down the hillside and are crowned by a small marble mausoleum, built as a tomb for the Marqués de la Quinta Roja. However, apparently his wife and mother disagreed about where to lay his body when he died, so the crypt was not used for its original purpose, and no one knows what (or who) lies within. (Plaza de la Constitución; free; 9am-8pm Mon-Fri, 9.30am-8.30pm Sat & Sun)

Iglesia de la Concepción
CHURCH

2 MAP P100, A4

This magnificent church, located right in the centre of town, dates to 1516, although it was destroyed by earthquakes in 1704 and 1705 and rebuilt in 1768. Today it is recognised as one of the finest examples of baroque architecture in the entire Canaries archipelago, with its three-fronted façade and three 24m-high bell towers.

The interior is awe-inspiring, with its profusion of carved wood-work, stonework and gorgeous stained glass. (www.concepcion orotava.info; Plaza Patricia García; 9am-8pm)

Iglesia de la Concepción

Museo de Artesanía Iberoamericana   MUSEUM

3 MAP P100, B2

Housed in the former Convento de Santo Domingo, the Museo de Artesanía Iberoamericana explores the cultural relationship between the Canaries and the Americas. Exhibits include a huge range of musical instruments, ceramics and various artefacts, many made in the countries of South America.

There's also an excellent gift shop with a splendid array of choice. (Iberoamerican Handicrafts Museum; Calle Tomás Zerolo 34; adult/child €2/free; 9am-6pm Mon-Fri, 9.30am-2pm Sat)

Beautiful Balconies

La Orotava has been very fortunate to preserve the beauty of its past. Traditional mansions are flanked with ornate wooden balconies like pirate galleons and surrounded by manicured gardens. You can cover the centre on foot in just half a day. Plaza de la Constitución, a large, shady plaza, is a good place to start exploring. On the plaza's northeastern side is the **Iglesia de San Agustín** (Map p100, C3; Plaza de la Constitución; hours vary), a simple church with a carved wooden ceiling.

Casa Lercaro   HISTORIC BUILDING

4 MAP P100, A4

This 16th-century mansion is widely considered to be the most representative building constructed in traditional Canary Island style. Particularly noteworthy is the finely carved baroque decoration on the woodwork, including the magnificent traditional balconies. The interior plant- and palm-filled courtyard is now a restaurant, while there's a decor shop and cafe too. (922 33 06 29; www.casalercaro.com; Calle del Colegio 5-7; restaurant 9am-7pm Mon-Thu, to 6.30pm Fri, 10am-midnight Sat)

Casa del Turista   HISTORIC BUILDING

5 MAP P100, A5

The building was a 16th-century convent and today houses an art gallery, a Tenerife pearl shop and an arts-and-crafts shop that includes a permanent display of a volcanic-sand carpet, typical of those produced for the Corpus Christi celebrations. (Calle San Francisco 4; 9am-6.30pm)

La Maquina   HISTORIC BUILDING

6 MAP P100, A4

Once the staple diet of the Guanches, *gofio* is essentially milled wheat and corn with the consistency of wholegrain flour. At this historic mill you can watch the miller at work grinding the grain, and buy a small bag of *gofio* (€1.50; raw or combined with cinnamon, chocolate or vanilla). You can also pick up an energy bar made of *gofio;* jars of honey are also for sale. (Molino de Gofio; ☎922 33 07 03; Calle del Colegio 3; ⏰8am-1pm & 2.30-6pm Sun-Fri, 9.30am-1pm Sat)

Museo de las Alfombras
MUSEUM

7 ◉ MAP P100, A5

This 'Museum of the Carpets' celebrates the town's Corpus Christi festival (p106) with its carpets created from flowers and coloured sands from El Teide. Set in a beautiful mansion dating from 1642, exhibits explain the history of the tradition, as well as the process. There is also a wonderfully atmospheric and grainy 10-minute black-and-white audiovisual presentation of past festivities. (Calle San Francisco 5; adult/child €2/free; ⏰10am-2pm Mon-Fri)

Hijuela del Botánico
GARDENS

8 ◉ MAP P100, B4

This small, sweet botanical garden centred around a magnificent *drago* (dragon) tree was created as a branch of the larger Jardín Botánico in Puerto de la Cruz. It is home to around 3000 labelled plant varieties – including a towering *Pino de Norfolk* – as well as plenty of birds, butterflies and strategically located benches. (Calle León; free; ⏰10am-3pm Mon-Fri)

Tackling El Teide

The **Parque Nacional del Teide Administrative Offices** (Map p100, A2; ☎922 92 23 71; www.reservasparquesnacionales.es; Calle Sixto Perera González 25; ⏰9am-2pm & 3.30-6pm Tue-Sun) are based in La Orotava. You can register here to climb the El Teide summit (p134). There's also an informative museum covering the geology, fauna and flora of the El Teide region, and an eight-minute film about the national park.

Eating

Bar la Duquesa
CANARIAN €

9 ✕ MAP P100, A4

Cooking since 1942, this friendly and popular family-run place has a pleasing interior of old photos, decorative gourds and farming utensils. The menu includes hearty local choices such as lentil stew, paella, grilled pork and salmon salad. There are outside tables on the cobbled road in the shadow of the church. (Plaza Patricio García 6; mains €6.50-8.50; ⏰7am-4pm Mon-Fri, 8am-3pm Sat)

Relieve Restaurant
BAKERY €

10 ✕ MAP P100, B4

With such adorable delights as blueberry tart, moist double-chocolate brownies, macaroons,

Menú del Día 🍽️

The traveller's friend in the Canary Islands, as in mainland Spain, is the *menú del día,* a set meal available at many restaurants for lunch and occasionally in the evening too. Generally, you get a starter (salad, soup or pasta) followed by a meat, fish or seafood main and a simple dessert, which can include local specialities or Spanish favourites such as *flan* (crème caramel), *helado* (ice cream), a piece of fruit or just a cup of coffee. Water, a glass of wine or a small draught beer may or may not be included. A *menú del día* will typically cost between around €10 and €12.

pastries and a wonderful selection of breads, this small but busy corner cafe and bakery is quite simply the best place in town for cakes and baked goodies. Try the speciality *patchanga,* a deliciously creamy custard-filled doughnut. There's also an ice-cream counter opening onto the street, and a decent tea selection.

All the baked goodies and desserts are labelled and priced, so choosing what you want is a doddle. (www.boutiquerelieve.com; Calle Carrera Escultor; cakes €0.80-2; ⏲7am-9.30pm)

Casa Egon   BAKERY €

11 🍴 MAP P100, B4

Established in 1916, this is the oldest *pasteleria* (cake shop) in the Canaries and has happily maintained its stuck-in-a-time-warp atmosphere with yellow paintwork, antique weighing scales, original floor tiles and woodwork, and much of the decor. The cakes include all-time local favourites like *anís*-based *roscos* and apple-filled *cabello de angel*. There is a simple, traditional restaurant out back. (Calle León 5; cakes €0.80-1; ⏲cake shop 10am-8.30pm Wed-Sun, to 4pm Tue, restaurant noon-8.30pm Wed-Sun)

Tapias La Bodega   SPANISH €

12 🍴 MAP P100, C3

Squeeze in with the locals at lunchtime and enjoy some hearty tapas at this atmospheric bar, with its barrel tables and large chalkboard menu over the bar. It's especially good for Basque-style *pintxos* (small pieces of bread topped with towering creations pinned in place with a toothpick), *bocadillos* (sandwich rolls) made with various seeded breads, and fresh salads. (📞922 33 53 95; Avenida de Canarias 6; pintxos €2.50, salads €6.50; ⏲8am-11pm)

Restaurante Victoria   INTERNATIONAL €€

13 🍴 MAP P100, B5

Dine at this superb restaurant in Hotel Rural Victoria's elegant atrium. There's exemplary presentation and flair in such dishes as duck confit with saffron, and the Canarian classic, rabbit in *salmorejo* (a marinade of bay leaves, garlic and wine) with *mojo* potatoes, as well as the *mus de gofio con almendras* (*gofio* mousse with almonds). (☏922 33 16 83; www.hotelruralvictoria.com; Calle Hermano Apolinar 8; mains €9-16; menú €11; ☺1-3.30pm & 7.30-9.30pm; ☏)

Tascafe Grimaldi   CANARIAN €€

14 ✖ MAP P100, A4

Swathed in tranquillity, the main terrace of this historic 1624 mansion, with its sea views, fountain and *drago* (dragon) tree, is the place to head on a balmy summer's evening. It's a laid-back cafe, bar and elegant restaurant rolled into one, with dishes including pumpkin soup, homemade croquettes, Canarian tuna fish with *mojo* and goat's-cheese salad with roasted peppers. (Casa Lercaro; ☏615 26 65 26; Calle del Colegio 7; mains €10-15; ☺10.30am-7pm Sun-Wed, to 11pm Thu & Fri)

Bodega el Reloj   CANARIAN €€

15 ✖ MAP P100 C6

This restaurant's beautiful setting, overlooking terraced gardens and verdant slopes to the sea, has a touch of Italy's Amalfi Coast about it. Dishes are as good to look at as they are to eat and include sharing platters, hot-stone-seared steaks or the fancier oxtail stew with truffled sweet potato. Take the

TF-21 around 3.5km southeast of La Orotava towards El Teide; it's signposted. (☏696 38 65 24; www.bodegaelreloj.es; Camino Los Frontones 37; mains €12-15; ☺1-4.30pm & 7.30-11pm Thu-Sat, 1-4.30pm Sun & Wed)

Sabor Canario   CANARIAN €€

16 ✖ MAP P100, B4

Exercise your taste buds with soul-satisfying traditional cuisine at this fabulous restaurant located in the lovely, leafy and light-filled patio of the Hotel Rural Orotava. The building – a wonderful old Canarian townhouse stuffed full of memorabilia – is very much part of the experience. A set vegetarian menu (€15 to €17) means noncarnivores are not excluded. (www.hotelruralorotava.es; Hotel Rural Orotava, Calle

Spanish *flan* (crème caramel)

La Orotava Eating

Corpus Christi

Corpus Christi is celebrated with extravagance in La Orotava (the date changes annually, but it's always in June), when an intricately designed, colourful floral carpet (made from petals, leaves and branches) is laid on the streets. In the Plaza de Ayuntamiento, a tapestry of biblical scenes is fashioned from El Teide coloured sands.

Carrera Escultor 17; mains €10-15; noon-3.30pm & 6-10pm Tue-Sat;)

Drinking

Liceo de Taoro BAR

17 MAP P100, C4

The 19th-century Liceo de Taoro has a magnificent setting high above the square. It's now a private club, where you can still order a drink from the bar within and take it to the front terrace overlooking the ornamental gardens, planted with birds of paradise and poinsettias, and the rooftops beyond. (922 33 01 19; www.liceodetaoro.es; 9am-11pm Mon-Sun)

Shopping

Canarias Concept ARTS & CRAFTS

18 MAP P100, A4

As the name implies, Canarias Concept sells solely Canarian-made crafts and products. It has a large showroom packed with jewellery, ceramics, artwork, handmade toys, ornaments, glazed tiles, soap, scarves and T-shirts, plus a gourmet section with goodies like palm honey, cactus-based spreads, *tortas de almendras* (almond biscuits) and local wines. (www.canariasconcept.com; Calle Carrera Escultor 23; 10am-7pm Mon-Sat)

MAIT ARTS & CRAFTS

In a former 17th-century convent, this museum shop (see 3 Map p100, B2) sells a great range of Ibero-American art and crafts, mainly from Central and South America. Ornaments and T-shirts from Mexico, Peruvian knitwear and nativity figures, Argentinian woven rugs, Colombian woven baskets, toys, jewellery and textiles are all displayed in a blaze of vivid colour in a spacious showroom. (Museo de Artesania Iberoamericana; 922 32 81 60; www.artenerife.com; Calle Tomás Zerolo 34; 9am-6pm Mon-Fri, 9.30am-2pm Sat)

Casa Torrehermosa ARTS & CRAFTS

19 MAP P100, B3

Tenerife's excellent art-and-crafts chain Artenerife has its local outlet in this magnificent 17th-mansion. Casa Torrehermosa provides a fitting setting for the display of locally produced artwork, pottery, jewellery and crafts, ranging from delicate hand-painted fans to sophisticated ceramics and glassware. Maps, posters and cards are

Floral carpet, Corpus Christi

also available. (📞922 33 32 99; www. artenerife.com; Calle Tomás Zerolo 27; 🕑10am-5pm Mon-Fri)

Depatanegra Ibericos
FOOD & DRINKS

20 🅰 MAP P100, C3

Carries a superb range of Spanish hams, including the highly desired *jamón iberico de bellota*, made from acorn-fed black pigs. Expect to pay around €16.50 per 100g. Hams are sold sliced up and vacuum-packed for easy packing. You'll also find a wide choice of chorizo, and a superb range of local wines, palm honey and Canarian and Spanish cheeses. (📞922 32 54 83; Avenida de Canarias 7; 🕑9am-9pm Mon-Fri, to 2.30pm Sat)

Encuentro
FASHION & ACCESSORIES

21 🅰 MAP P100, C3

The women's fashions here are sharp, sassy and inexpensive, with an emphasis on informal designs, colourful prints and natural fabrics. The regular sales ensure that nothing hangs around for too long. (📞922 33 47 69; www.encuentro moda.es; Calle Calvario 5; 🕑9.30am-9pm Mon-Sat)

Explore ◈

Los Cristianos

Full of contradictions, Los Cristianos has, on the one hand, a kiss-me-quick reputation of karaoke bars and all-day English breakfasts. On the other, it is known for its superb city beach and water sports, its quirky independent shops, its great seafood and a small traditional centre, which still reflects a semblance of Canarian character with old-time bars.

The Short List

○ **Puerto de Los Cristianos (p110)** *Setting off to sail, dive or fish from the harbour or simply watching the boats come and go.*

○ **Playa de Los Cristianos (p115)** *Settling down on the sand, joining with a game of volleyball or cooling down with a nice cold beer in a beachfront bar.*

○ **El Cine (p116)** *Polishing off a simple fish-based feast among throngs of cheery local diners.*

Getting There & Around

🚗 There are taxi stands outside most shopping centres.

🚌 Most of the long-distance-bus routes serve as local routes. Bus 111 (indirect, €9.45) comes and goes from Santa Cruz, travelling via Tenerife Sur Airport (€9.35).

⚓ Ferries depart from the ferry terminal for the neighbouring islands of La Gomera, El Hierro and La Palma.

Los Cristianos Map on p114

View over Los Cristianos PRISCILA GONZALEZ/SHUTTERSTOCK ©

Top Experience 📷
Puerto de Los Cristianos

Playa de Los Cristianos' golden sand is flanked to the east by Puerto de Los Cristianos, a harbour that's home to fishing boats, private yachts and commercial boats offering everything from boat rides to big-game-fishing trips. Waters here drop to dramatic depths and the combination of caves, a temperate climate and diverse ocean life create ideal conditions for diving. Windsurfing and kitesurfing are also popular, as well paddling in the sea.

◎ MAP P114, C4

Try Dive

Consider Los Cristianos for your first diving experience. Not only are the waters an agreeable temperature, but the coast is sheltered from the waves and winds that can blast the northern resorts. There are no coral reefs, but you can expect to see barracuda, stingrays and morays among the larger sea life, and shoals of triggerfish and rainbow wrasse among the smaller fry. Snorkelling is another popular option.

Boat Trips

Most people find that the dolphin- and whale-watching trips are worth the euro (vegetarians may get peckish though; most include a meat-only barbecue), as you are virtually guaranteed to spot the mammals. A glass-bottom boat can add to the experience. There are several tour-company kiosks located in the harbour.

Ferries

OK, it's not strictly a sport, but consider cruising the waters between Tenerife and La Gomera in a ferry, enjoying the view from the deck and leaving the stunning outline of El Teide behind you. You can reach here in less than an hour. La Gomera is also the island that has best preserved its culture, so presenting an interesting contrast to Tenerife's southern resorts.

Nearby: El Médano

Located 21km east of Los Cristianos and not yet squashed by steamroller development, El Médano is a world-class spot for windsurfers and kitesurfers, and their sails speckle the horizon like exotic butterfly wings. Water sports companies and rental outfits are mainly located near the beach, all 2km of it – the longest in Tenerife.

★ Top Tips

o For more water sports ideas, check out the flyers at the tourist office, ask for recommendations and visit www. webtenerife.com.

o Surfers will find the best waves between February and March; the calmest waters for scuba divers are in July and August.

o Look out for red flags indicating that conditions are unsafe for swimming.

✕ Take a Break

o The most obvious cuisine in Los Cristianos is seafood, and one of the best places to find the flapping freshest is at the kiosks on the harbour.

o Alternatively, excellent El Cine (p116) offers culinary symphonies of fishy fare.

Walking Tour 🥾

Backstreet Los Cristianos

Step back from the tourist-clogged beachfront to discover a part of town that still has a fishing-village feel, with old-fashioned bars, idiosyncratic small shops, and an overall pueblo buzz with benches and squares for kicking-back time. Discover where the locals go for seafood and entertainment: it's a far cry from fish and chips and karaoke.

Walk Facts

Start Sopa
End Pescaderia Dominga
Length 0.8km; 1½ hours

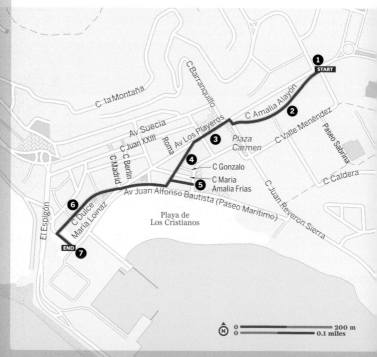

❶ Sopa Sofa Breakfast

Chilled-out **Sopa** (p117) is strewn with sofas, comfy armchairs and shelves of books and magazines, providing the backdrop for a (largely vegetarian) menu of healthy soups, salads and burgers (spinach, that is). There are also delicious cakes. Try the cherry and marzipan for a real taste-bud treat. The orange juice, coffee and tomato on toast (€3) is a steal for snackers.

❷ Time for Tea

Stop by **La Cabaña del Té** (p119), a temple to tea, where the shelves are filled with colourful tins of every imaginable brew. You'll find combinations that you won't get elsewhere, such as pineapple with aloe vera and *flor de cactus* (cactus flower) and banana. You'll be able to try a cup while you browse.

❸ Traditional Canarian Bar

Opposite the grand church Nuestra Señora del Carmen and one of the most atmospheric and buzzing-with-locals squares in town, **Bar Gavota** (p118) is a perennial favourite that has retained its typical Spanish feel and faithful crowd of regulars. It's perfect for an inexpensive traditional tapa, like a generous wedge of moist tortilla, or homemade *croquetas*.

❹ Family-Run Bookshop

A literary fixture, the bookshop **Librería Barbara** (p120) was founded in 1984 and supplies avid readers with new and secondhand books in a medley of languages, a reflection of the diverse nationalities of Los Cristianos' visitors. It's a lovely place for a browse and a spot of book-hunting.

❺ Arts & Crafts

In a stand-alone, detached unit right by the sand, **La Alpizpa** (p119) displays a tremendous range of locally produced arts and crafts that make for imaginative souvenirs.

❻ Tapas Time

Stuffed away down a quiet back street, buzzing **La Tapa** (p117) is a local mainstay. There are 22 tapa choices, including some traditional homestyle favourites such as *callos con garbanzos* (tripe with chickpeas), *sopa de pollo* (chicken soup), plus *pescado frito* (fried seafood), *albondigas* (meatballs), potatoes with aioli (garlic mayonnaise)... the list goes on.

❼ Catch of the Day

Watertront kiosk **Pescadería Dominga** (p118) sells fresh-off-the-boat fish. You can take it home to cook yourself, or they will fry it up for you. If you choose the latter, you can sit on the jetty with what is likely to be the best and freshest fish picnic you'll ever have,

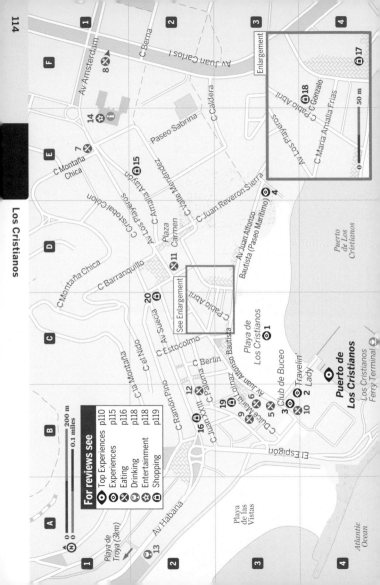

Los Cristianos

For reviews see
◉ Top Experiences p110
◉ Experiences p115
✕ Eating p116
🍷 Drinking p118
🎭 Entertainment p118
🛍 Shopping p119

0 ⟍ 200 m
0 ⟍ 0.1 miles

Playa de Troya (3km)

Av Habana

Playa de las Vistas

Atlantic Ocean

Puerto de Los Cristianos

Los Cristianos Ferry Terminal

Playa de Los Cristianos

Club de Buceo

El Espigón

Av Amsterdam

C Berna

Av Juan Carlos I

Paseo Sabrina

C Caldera

C Montaña Chica

C Cristóbal Colón

Av Los Playeros

C Amalia Alayón

Plaza Carmen

C Valle Menéndez

C Juan Reverón Sierra

Av Juan Alfonso Bautista (Paseo Marítimo)

C Pablo Abril

C Estocolmo

C Barranquillo

C el Nido

Av Suecia

C la Montaña

C Montaña Chica

C Ramón Pino

C Berlín

C Paloma

Av Juan Alfonso Bautista

C Dulce María Loynaz

C Juan XXIII

Enlargement

C Pablo Abril

C Gonzalo

C María Amalia Frías

0 ⟍ 50 m

Puerto de Los Cristianos

Experiences

Playa de Los Cristianos

BEACH

1 MAP P114, C3

This 1km-long taupe-coloured sandy stretch is the main beach in town and is very family friendly, with a lifeguard, rows of sunbeds, volleyball net, bars, restaurants and ice-cream kiosks.

Travelin' Lady

BOATING

2 MAP P114, B3

Organises two-hour whale-watching trips and uses an enclosed propeller to prevent any injury to the mammals. Private charters are also available (640 531122; www. travelinladytenerife.com; Puerto de Los Cristianos; adult/child €25/10; ⏰9.30am-5pm Mon-Sat)

Club de Buceo

DIVING

3 MAP P114, B3

Operates out of a Puerto de Los Cristianos kiosk and offers a wide choice of dives, including the introductory 'try dive' for absolute beginners. (922 79 73 61; www. divingaronatenerife.es; Rincon de Arona, Puerto de Los Cristianos; dive incl equipment €60; ⏰9am-6pm)

Escuela de Vela Los Cristianos

WINDSURFING, BOATING

4 MAP P114, E3

Head to the far east of the beach at Los Cristianos where this popular local sailing school is located. It rents out windsurfers, as well

Playa de Los Cristianos

Know Your South-Coast Beaches

Tenerife's south-coast beaches come complete with mojito-mixing beach bars and chic restaurants; for something more low key, however, head to the beaches at the nearby towns of Las Galletas (p126) and El Médano (p111).

Playa de Los Cristianos (p115) The main beach in town (1km-long) is perfect for family outings, with a lifeguard on duty, and a range of bars and restaurants, as well as ice-cream kiosks. Sunbeds and a volleyball net are available.

Playa de las Vistas (p126) A sublime 1.5km-long beach lined with bars and restaurants, with fine golden sand that was imported from the Sahara Desert! Protected by breakwaters, it is perfect for swimming.

Playa de Troya (Playa de las Américas) One of several beaches that merge seamlessly into each other in central Playa, with soft dark sand and excellent facilities.

Playa del Duque (p126) 'Duke's Beach' (600m-long) is an attractive golden sandy beach fringed with cheerful changing huts, and stylish cafes and restaurants.

Playa de la Enramada (La Caleta, Costa Adeje) A dark volcanic beach with a great beach bar; a popular launch spot for hang-gliding.

as offering courses (from €50 for two hours), and also has Laser sailing boats for hire. (☑610 80 12 00; Avenida Chayofita 12, Playa de Los Cristianos; ☺10.30am-5pm Mon-Fri, to 2pm Sat & Sun; 🚹)

Eating

El Cine   SEAFOOD €

5 ❌ MAP P114, B3

It's probably been said before, but El Cine deserves a medal for its inexpensive, simply prepared seafood. It's been here since the '80s, with a menu that's reassuringly

brief; the fish of the day is always a good bet. The no-frills atmosphere and few tourists only adds to the appeal. It's tucked away in an elbow off the promenade and off the drag. (☑609 107758; www. grupoelcine.com/restaurante-el-cine; Calle Juan Bariajo 8; mains €7.50-13; ☺11.30am-11pm)

Il Gelato del Mercado   GELATO €

6 ❌ MAP P114, B3

This enterprising and popular hole-in-the-wall *gelateria* sells tubs and cones of superb gelato, concocted with natural and locally sourced ingredients, to help cool off under the fierce Los Cristianos sun. Gelato comes in four sizes: *mini, piccolo, medio* and *grande*. (Calle Dulce María LoInaz 1; gelato €1-3; ⏱1-10pm Mon-Thu, noon-11pm Fri & Sat, noon-10pm Sun)

Sopa INTERNATIONAL €

7 🍴 MAP P114, E1

This chilled-out space with sofas, armchairs, and books and magazines for you to enjoy, serves a (mostly vegetarian) menu of soups, salads and spinach burgers, as well as excellent cakes, such as a delicious cherry and marzipan. If you're looking for a quick snack, orange juice, coffee and tomato on toast (€3) is great value. (📞822 04 37 69; Calle Montaña Chica 2; salads & soups €4-7; ⏱8am-8pm Mon-Sat, 8.30am-5pm Sun; 📶🍴)

La Pepa Food Market MARKET €

8 🍴 MAP P114, F1

This gourmet food market has stalls including delis, a seafood counter, sushi, a pancakes and waffles stand, a wine bar and a vegetarian snack stall. There is plenty of seating on a vast terrace, with rooftop views that stretch to the sea, plus there's a children's playground. (📞922 79 48 85; Centro Comercial La Pasarela; snacks €2.50-5; ⏱10am-11pm Mon-Thu, to midnight Fri-Sun; 📶)

La Tapa TAPAS €

9 🍴 MAP P114, B3

Much loved by locals, buzzing La Tapa is appropriately (if unexcitingly) named, with 22 choices, including some traditional homestyle favourites such as tripe with chickpeas and chicken soup, plus fried seafood, prawns in garlic,

Los Cristianos Eating

Vegetarian and Vegan Dining 🍽

The Canary Islands may seem like paradise to some, but they can be hard going for vegetarians, and harder still for vegans. Although this is meat-eating country and you will find your choices (unless you self-cater) a little limited, there is a growing range of options and a growing number of flexitarian choices too.

Salads are a staple, and you will come across various side dishes such as *champiñones* (mushrooms; usually lightly fried in olive oil and garlic) and *berenjenas* (aubergines). Other possibilities include *menestra* (a hearty vegetable stew), *pimientos de padrón* (small grilled peppers sprinkled with rock salt) and, of course, the ubiquitous *papas* (potatoes). Some dishes that you might expect to be vegetarian – like stews made with *garbanzos* (chickpeas) or *lentejas* (lentils) – have often been cooked with meat, so it's best to ask before ordering.

Los Cristianos After Dark

Postmidnight, Los Cristianos' main action takes place at the Centro Comercial San Telmo, the shopping centre behind Playa de las Vistas, when this daytime-dull little strip is transformed into a string of nightclubs pumping out music late into the night. Look elsewhere if you're seeking somewhere classier; the number of alternatives is increasing all the time.

meatballs, potatoes with aioli and much more. (Calle Dulce María Loinaz; tapas €3.50; ⏰noon-midnight Wed-Mon)

Pescadería Dominga   SEAFOOD €

10 🍴 MAP P114, B3

On the waterfront in Los Cristianos' port area, ever-popular Pescadería Dominga (along with a handful of other kiosks) sells fresh fish. Take it away to cook at your leisure, or have them fry it up for you so you can feast on the pier while gazing out onto the sea. (Puerto de Los Cristianos; fish €5-9; ⏰noon-7pm Mon-Fri, to 3pm Sat)

Bar Gavota   CAFE €

11 🍴 MAP P114, D2

Opposite the church on the square in Los Cristianos, this is one of the few central bars here that retains its typical, traditional Spanish feel,

as well as a local crowd of regulars. It's perfect for a toast-and-coffee breakfast or drinks. (Avenida los Playeros 27; breakfast €5; ⏰8am-11pm Mon-Sat)

La Paloma   SPANISH €€

12 🍴 MAP P114, B2

Dating from 1969, this place rarely disappoints. Don't be put off by the multilingual menus – the food is resoundingly Spanish, with favourites like Andalucian gazpacho, Canarian rabbit *en salmorejo* (a marinade of bay leaves, garlic and wine), Valencian-style paella and plenty of tapas choice. (📞922 79 01 98; Calle Paloma 7; mains €10-16; ⏰11am-midnight Wed-Mon)

Drinking

Casablanca   CLUB

13 🍺 MAP P114, A2

A long-standing club at the western end of the Centro Comercial San Telmo. (Centro Comercial San Telmo; ⏰10pm-4am)

Entertainment

Centro Cultural   THEATRE

14 🌟 MAP P114, F8

Has a variety of cultural events, such as Cine de Verano, a summer festival of open-air movies (in Spanish) that show nightly except on Wednesdays. An auditorium acts as a concert venue. (www.centrocultural-cristiano.org; Plaza Pescador 1)

Shopping

La Cabaña del Té

TEA

15  MAP P114, F8

If you're a tea drinker, stop by this temple to the tea leaf, which offers an extensive range of teas, presented in traditional metal tins. Flavours include pineapple with aloe vera, *flor de cactus* (cactus flower) and banana. Enjoy a cuppa while you browse. (Calle Amalia Alayón 20; ⏰10am-2pm & 5-8.30pm Mon-Fri, 10am-2pm Sat)

Jamón y Mojo

FOOD & DRINKS

16 MAP P114, E8

Run by an enthusiastic young couple, this deli has a vast range of carefully sourced gourmet products, with an emphasis on Spanish delights, such as great wheels of crumbly Manchego cheese and several grades of chorizo and *jamón serrano* (Serrano ham). They also make superb sandwiches and carry an extensive selection of wines. (📞674 736901; Avenida Suecia 35; ⏰10am-11pm)

La Alpizpa

ARTS & CRAFTS

17 MAP P114 F8

Right on the seafront and standing all by itself, this shop sells an eye-catching range of high-quality and diverse arts and crafts made by people with disabilities, as well as local produce such as *mojo* (Canarian spicy sauce) and liqueurs. (Avenida Juan Alfonso Batista; ⏰10.25am-8.15pm Tue, Thu, Fri & Sat, 11am-8.15pm Wed, 11am-4pm Sun & Mon)

Los Cristianos Harbour

Librería Barbara

BOOKS

18 🔒 MAP P114, F8

A literary fixture, this bookshop was founded in 1984 and supplies avid readers with new and secondhand books in a medley of languages, plus magazines and children's titles. (📞922 79 23 01; Calle Pablo Abril 6; 🕙10am-1.30pm & 5-8pm Mon-Fri, 10am-1.30pm Sat)

Tina

FASHION & ACCESSORIES

19 🔒 MAP P114, B3

If you like bling, leopard-skin prints (on everything from wellington boots to umbrellas), killer-heel shoes or gold lamé frocks, be sure to check out Tina. This entertainingly original boutique is reputed to have been the first to open here back in the '70s. (Calle Dulce María Loinaz 10; 🕙10am-1pm & 5-8pm Mon-Fri, 10am-1pm Sat)

Pesquera y Navales Tenerife

SPORTS & OUTDOORS

20 🔒 MAP P114, E8

If you fancy dropping a line and sinker, or investing in some thigh-high wellies (in secret or otherwise), or if you just want to browse through the piled-high shelves of every kind of product, item of clothing or seafaring souvenir related to fishing, then this is the shop for you. (📞922 79 79 11; www.pesquerasynavales.com; Calle Dulce María Loinaz; 🕙8am-1pm & 4-9pm Mon-Fri, to 1pm Sat)

Pilot whales

Tenerife Wildlife

There is wildlife out there, but it tends to be small, shy and largely undetectable to the untrained eye. Lizards and birds are the biggest things you'll see. There are around 200 species of bird on the Canary Islands, though many are imports from Africa and Europe. And yes, before you ask, this is where canaries come from, but the wild cousins are of a much duller colour than the popular cage birds.

If it's big animals you want, you need to get off land and turn to the ocean. The stretch of water between Tenerife and La Gomera is a traditional feeding ground for as many as 26 species of whale, and others pass through during migration. The most common are pilot whales, sperm whales and bottlenose dolphins.

Whale-watching is big business around here, and 800,000 people a year head out on boats to get a look. A law regulates observation of sea mammals, prohibiting boats from getting closer than 60m to an animal and limiting the number of boats following pods at any one time. The law also tries to curb practices such as using sonar and other devices to attract whales' attention. If you decide to take a whale-watching tour, join up with a reputable company.

Blazers

FASHION & ACCESSORIES

21 🔒 MAP P114, C2

A refreshing change from the humdrum fashions aimed at souvenir-hoarding tourists (such as slogan-blazoned T-shirts and overpriced swimwear), this eye-catching Los Cristianos boutique has a fun, youthful edge with its collection of slinky dresses with intricate lacework; it also has a selection of more informal wear. (📞 922 79 31 94; Calle Juan XXIII; 🕐 10.30am-1.30pm & 5-8.30pm Mon-Fri, 10.30am-1.30pm & 5.30-8.30pm Sat)

Explore ◉

Playa de las Américas & Costa Adeje

It's easy to get sniffy about Playa de las Américas and, while its reputation for sun-kissed holidays for the masses is well earned, it's not what it used to be. True, the resort is still 100% tourist driven, but there is a sophisticated sheen to the place now which is especially evident in the bars, restaurants and overall nightlife that seem to merge seamlessly with the adjacent, upmarket Costa Adeje.

The Short List

○ **Playa de las Vistas (p126)** Taking a dip in the Atlantic to cool down after a stint of sunbathing on the sand.

○ **Bar el Pincho (p130)** Sipping on cocktails as you watch the world go by at this beachfront bar.

○ **Siam Park (p126)** Treating the kids to an afternoon of cheesy fun in the region's largest theme park.

Getting There & Around

🚗 There are taxi stands outside most shopping centres.

🚌 Most of the long-distance-bus routes serve double duty as local routes, stopping along the major avenues of Playa de las Américas before heading elsewhere. Bus 111 (indirect, €9.45) comes and goes from Santa Cruz, travelling via Tenerife Sur Airport (€9.35).

Playa de las Américas & Costa Adeje Map on p124

For reviews see

Experiences	p126
Eating	p128
Drinking	p130
Entertainment	p132
Shopping	p132

Playa de las Américas & Costa Adeje

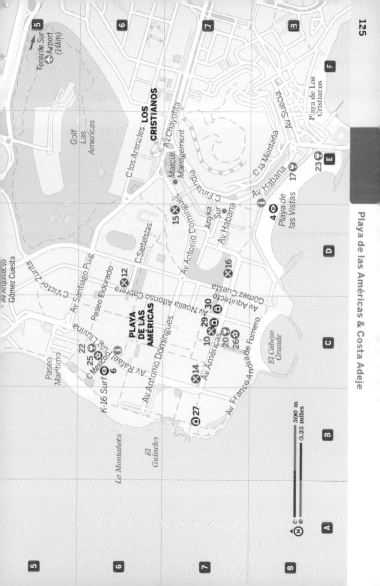

Playa de las Américas & Costa Adeje

LOS CRISTIANOS

Golf
Las
Américas

Tenerife Sur
Airport
(14km) **5**

C los Arenales

Av Chayofita

Marcus
Chayofita
Management

C Finlandia

Anyka
Sur

Av Habana

Av Suecia

Playa de Los
Cristianos

C la Montaña

Playa de
las Vistas

17

23

E

15

D

16

Av Antonio Domingo

Av Aquitecto
Gómez Cuesta

C Siete Islas

12

Paseo Eldorado

Av Santiago Puig

Av Victor Zurita

Av Arquitecto
Gómez Cuesta

Paseo
Marítimo

La Montañeta

El
Guincho

K-16 Surf

C Luz Livina

C Rafael Domingo

22

25

6

**PLAYA
DE LAS
AMÉRICAS**

Av Antonio Domingues

Av Noelia Alfonso Cabrera

29 30

10

20

26

Av Américas

14

27

Av Franco Andrade Fumero

El Cabezo
Grande

500 m
0.25 miles

A   **B**   **C**

5   **6**   **7**   **8**

Experiences

Siam Park
AMUSEMENT PARK

1 MAP P124, D3

Southern Tenerife's biggest theme park is the impressive Siam Park, which offers a chance to throw yourself down a 28m-high vertical water slide, surf in a swimming pool, get spat out of the guts of a dragon and buy tat at a Bangkok-style floating market. Entry for tots under three is free. (📞 902 06 00 00; www.siampark.net; Autopista Sur, exit 28, Costa Adeje; adult/child €37/25; ⏰ 10am-6pm May-Oct, to 5pm Nov-Apr; 🅿)

La Caleta
AREA

2 MAP P124, C1

This resort area in Costa Adeje is located north of Playa del Duque and is anchored by several hotels, including the Sheraton La Caleta Resort and Spa. The main beach is Playa de la Enramada (p116), a length of black volcanic sand; you can also find the Mirador Stone Pebble Beach here, where visitors have piled up hundreds of pebble columns, making for excellent photos at sunset.

Playa del Duque
BEACH

3 MAP P124, C1

The appealing 600m-long 'Duke's beach' is a golden sandy stretch backed by jaunty striped changing huts, chic cafes and restaurants. (Costa Adeje)

Playa de las Vistas
BEACH

4 MAP P124, D8

This sublime 1.5km-long beach has fine golden sand (imported from the Sahara Desert!) and links Los Cristianos with Playa de las Américas. The beach is backed by bars and restaurants and protected by breakwaters, so it's ideal for swimming. (Playa de las Américas)

Neptuno
BOATING

5 MAP P124, B2

This reputable company organises several boat tours, including a five-hour excursion on a traditional teak-hardwood sailing ship called *Shogun* (formerly owned by a sheikh), during which you are almost guaranteed to see dolphins and whales. It also includes an option to swim in the bay of Masca and enjoy a traditional paella lunch. A complimentary hotel shuttle

---

A Bit of Quiet in Las Galletas

Las Galletas is a small resort town a few kilometres south of the Las Américas strip and, in comparison, is as quiet as a Sunday afternoon in a library; for many people that is its attraction. A block back from the boardwalk, the leafy Rambla Dionisio González, with benches and playgrounds, leads to the tourist office and the sea.

K-16 Surf SURFING

6 ⊙ MAP P124, C6

This school hires out surfboards and provides tuition for only slightly more than the price of rental. For newbies, group surf initiation lessons are two hours (€35), a full course of five lessons is €150, and private surf lessons start at €70 for two hours. Kids and people with disabilities are also catered for. K-16 Surf sells skateboards and has two nearby surf shops. (📞922 78 87 79; https://k16surf.com; Calle México 22, Playa de las Américas; surf lessons from €35, board rental per day from €15; 👶)

...rvice is available. (📞922 79 80 44; www.barcostenerife.com; Calle Colón, Puerto Colón, Costa Adeje; 3hr boat tour adult/child €39/19.50; ⊙9am-9pm)

Vitanova Spa SPA

7 ⊙ MAP P124, C1

This spa offers massages and facials as well as scrumptious delights, such as a chocolate massage, an anticellulite scrub with seaweed and grapes, and a Dead Sea mud wrap. (📞922 71 99 10; www.vitanovatenerife.com; Calle Alcalde Walter Paetzman, Playa del Duque, Costa Adeje; ⊙11am-9pm)

La Caldera del Rey HORSE RIDING

8 ⊙ MAP P124, E2

Located on a traditional Canarian farm in San Eugenio Alto, this excellent riding stable also has a children's petting farm, barbecue area, climbing wall and a low rope course for children. (📞648 650441;

Playa de las Americas

The South Coast with Kids

There is loads going on for children of all ages here. Along the beaches, carnival-like attractions such as bumper cars and mini bungee jumping are popular with older kids, while playgrounds on Playa de Los Cristianos and behind the Centro Comercial in Los Cristianos can keep the little ones entertained.

Kids' surfing lessons can easily take care of several hours and teach the young ones a whole new set of exciting skills, while potentially sowing the seeds for a lifelong enthusiasm for tube-riding and turtle-rolling.

Away from the beaches, there are theme parks, and water slides and pools galore. All parks have free bus services.

Avenida Francia, Costa Adeje; 2hr trek €50; ⏰9am-8.30pm; 🚻)

Eating

Otelo   CANARIAN €

9 🍴 MAP P124 C1

This Adeje restaurant is primarily about its dramatic views over the Barranco del Infierno, but the Canarian menu is very good too; the mainstay is Otelo's chicken in garlic (€4.95), but there's also *conejo al salmorejo* (rabbit in *salmorejo,* a marinade of bay leaves, garlic and wine), fillet steak in mushroom sauce and other crowd-pleasing fare. It's a good choice for calorific boosting before, or after, your hike. (📞922 78 03 74; Calle de los Molinos 44, Costa Adeje; mains €4.95-15; ⏰11am-10.30pm)

Thai Botanico   THAI €€

10 🍴 MAP P124, C7

This enchanting choice is decorated with sumptuous decor and serves a large choice of well-crafted Thai dishes. Curries, stir-fries, salads, spring rolls, satay dishes and pad thai noodles...all the Thai favourites are here, well presented and delicately enhanced with fragrant herbs and aromatic spices. Reservations are essential. (📞922 79 77 59; www.thaibotanicotenerife.com; Commercial Centre Safari, 1st fl, Avenida Américas, Playa de las Américas; mains €7.50-17; ⏰1.30-11.30pm Mon-Sat, 6.30-11pm Sun; 🛜)

Café La Bahia   CAFE €€

11 🍴 MAP P124, C1

Draw up a chair at this French Riviera–like cafe with its giant sun umbrellas, Med-blue tablecloths and waiters wearing boaters, and choose between a coffee, *cerveza* (beer) or ice cream. Light meals are also available. (Playa del Duque, Costa Adeje; mains €12-15; ⏰10am-10pm)

Mesón Las Lanzas   SPANISH €€

12 🍴 MAP P124, D6

Hurray. No sunbleached photos of chips-with-everything 'international' dishes on the pavement. Instead come here to enjoy traditional Spanish mains like *tigres* (deep-fried mussels), fresh fish of the day, roast shoulder of lamb or rabbit in *salmorejo*. The preparation is simplicity itself, just fresh and homely cuisine – don't miss it. (☏922 79 11 72; www.mesonlaslanzas.com; Avenida Noelia Alfonso Cabrera 8, Playa de las Américas; mains €7.50-18; ☺1-4pm & 7pm-midnight)

La Torre del Mirador CANARIAN €€

13 ✖ MAP P124, C1

This elegant bar and restaurant has a lovely terrace with colourful flowers and palms and delightful sea views. The menu has several sound seafood choices, including king prawns in garlic and tuna cooked with onions. Or share a platter of *pimientos de padron* (small fried green peppers), the perfect accompaniment to a long cold *cerveza* after your promenade stroll. (☏922 71 22 09; www.latorredelmirador.com; Playa del Duque, Costa Adeje; mains €12-16; ☺12.30am-11.30pm Wed-Mon)

Bianco Restaurant ITALIAN €€

14 ✖ MAP P124, C7

Munch on thin-crust pizzas (opt for one of the gourmet varieties) and house-made pastas at this shorefront restaurant with its dazzling white decor and elegant, if somewhat dated, atmosphere. If you're not in the mood for *Italiano*,

The Future of Tourism

The classic double-edged sword, tourism continues to represent an essential pillar of the economy of the Canary Islands, with over 32% of Canarian economic activity linked to it. More than 14 million visitors passed through the islands in 2017, with the majority heading to a single island: Tenerife. But with almost 40% of visitors to the Canary Islands in 2016 arriving from the UK, Brexit storm clouds have been darkening economic predictions, especially as the slumping British pound took the wind from British travellers' sails in 2018.

The fear of British holidaymakers saying *adiós* to the Canary Islands prompted the local government to consider sweeteners such as exempting British holidaymakers from paying IGIC (Canary Indirect General Tax). It is estimated the move – if it comes into effect – could cost around €100 million a year, but is considered to be money well spent. Elsewhere, however, there are signs that overtourism could be becoming a problem. A sustainable-tourism tax could be in the offing too, similar to the tax recently introduced by the Balearic Islands to help control visitor numbers and provide money for environmental protection and heritage conservation.

Papas Arrugadas 🍽️

By a long chalk, the most-often-spotted Canarian dish is *papas arrugadas* (wrinkly potatoes), cooked in an abundance of salt and always served with some variation of *mojo* (Canarian spicy sauce made from coriander, basil or red chilli peppers).

alternatives include fillet steak (with foie gras), salmon or salt-baked chicken. The *zeppoli* (dough balls) starter has received rave reviews from diners. (📞922 78 86 97; www.biancorestauranttenerife.com; Avenida Américas 5, Playa de las Américas; mains €7.50-25; 🕐1-11pm; 📶)

Gastrobar La Kocina SPANISH €€

15 🍴 MAP P124, D7

A slick contemporary interior is the appropriate setting for enjoying pretty-as-a-picture tapas. Enticing dishes include grilled fresh tuna, and Spanish prime beef entrecôte. (📞922 79 46 30; Avenida Antonio Domínguez, Playa de las Américas; mains €9-17; 🕐1-4pm & 7-11pm; 📶)

Oriental Monkey ASIAN €€€

16 🍴 MAP P124, D7

This gourmet restaurant combines exotic decor with an exotic menu of innovatively prepared Asian-inspired dishes, ranging from red tuna with *yuzukoshō,* avocado and coriander, to beef *tataki* with jalapeño peppers

and teriyaki sauce, or tartar of snow crab with kimchi mayonnaise, all prepared in an open kitchen.

Expect an entertaining evening, with video projections of pink butterflies flying across your table, or fish swimming across your plate, while muted coloured lights constantly shift and change. (📞922 78 92 91; www.theorientalmonkey.com; Avenida de las Américas, Central Comercial Oasis, Playa de las Américas; mains €14-25; 🕐7-11.30pm Mon-Sat; 📶)

Drinking

Bar el Pincho BAR

17 🍺 MAP P124, E8

Come to bright-white-painted Bar el Pincho for a cocktail (€6) or gin and tonic (€6) at sunset. The mango daiquiris are the ideal accompaniment to the uninterrupted sand-and-sea views from the terrace above the boardwalk; the music's ace, too. During the day it's also an excellent choice for tapas, a coffee or a banana split (€6). (📞922 79 77 19; Playa de las Vistas, Playa de las Américas; 🕐10.30am-9pm Mon-Sat)

Papagayo BAR, CLUB

18 🍺 MAP P124, C4

This neat-looking restaurant, bar and nightclub oozes sophistication and good taste. There is kick-back seating facing the sunset, and a menu that's best for light dishes such as sushi. Come night-time the place shifts into fashionable nightclub mode, complete with slick professional DJs.

There's a €10 cover charge to dance on Friday, Saturday and Sunday nights. (www.papagayobeachclub.com; Avenida Rafael Puig Lluvina, Playa de las Américas; ☺10am-late; 📶)

Chiringuito Coqueluche
BAR

19 🚍 MAP P124, C1

Stroll along the promenade, past luxurious hotel gardens and around a small headland to the attractive dark-pebble beach of La Enramada, where you can sip a drink at the cheerful local beach bar. (Playa La Enramada, Costa Adeje; ☺10am-11pm)

Hard Rock Cafe
BAR

20 🚍 MAP P124, C7

Part of the worldwide rock and roll chain, with a buzzy vibe, music-themed decor and a stunning rooftop terrace with sea views beyond the palms. Regular live concerts and DJ sessions are held; check the calendar on the website. (📞922 05 50 22; www.hardrock.com; Avenida Américas, Playa de las Américas; ☺noon-12.30am; 📶)

Monkey Beach Club
CLUB

21 🚍 MAP P124, C4

Right on the beachfront at Playa de Troya, this is a winning spot for a sundowner and gradually fills up with a hip, good-looking crowd who gather here to drink, flirt and hit the strobe-lit dance floor. Some turn up earlier for a bite to eat. (📞922 78 92 91; www.grupomonkey.com; Avenida Rafael Puig Lluvina 3, Playa de las Américas; ☺11am-late; 📶)

Early morning, Playa de las Americas

Dubliner   IRISH PUB

22 🚻 MAP P124, C6

This Irish pub has Guinness on tap and nightly live music provided by the accomplished resident band. (📞922 79 39 03; Hotel Las Palmeras, Avenida Rafael Puig Lluvina, Playa de las Américas; ⏰9pm-5am; 📶)

Kiosco San Telmo   BAR

23 🚻 MAP P124, E8

This simple place has all it needs to whip up a killer mojito. Perch on a stool for some beachside magic. (Playa de las Vistas, Playa de las Américas; ⏰9am-6pm)

Chiringuito del Mirador   BAR

24 🚻 MAP P124, C1

This beach bar (and restaurant) is a lovely place for a midday cocktail or *cerveza,* accompanied by a plate of *gambas a la plancha* (grilled prawns) to share. (Playa del Duque, Costa Adeje; ⏰noon-7pm)

Entertainment
Sax Bar   LIVE MUSIC

25 ⭐ MAP P124, C6

If you like it loud, you like to rock and you are not averse to a mainly British clientele, then Sax may just well be your nightly boogie fix. Playing every night, the resident bands are up there with the best. (📞680 83 14 88; Calle Mexico, Playa de las Américas; ⏰9pm-2am)

La Pirámide   LIVE MUSIC

26 ⭐ MAP P124, C7

This vast auditorium regularly stages world-class shows that typically combine flamenco, opera and dance. You can combine the show with a buffet dinner (from €79), with dining times set at 6.30pm and 7pm. However, the food is decidedly less impressive than the show. (📞922 75 75 49; www.piramidearona.com; Avenida Américas, Playa de las Américas; tickets from €49; ⏰8pm Wed, 9pm Tue & Thu-Sun)

Shopping
Rip Curl   SPORTS & OUTDOORS

27 🛍 MAP P124, B7

Surf clothing and watches, wetsuits and shades: all your water-sport requirements are provided for here. The shop is affiliated with the surf school K-16 Surf (p127) just up the road, so enquire about surfing

---

Tap or Bottle? ⓘ

Much of the tap water found throughout the Canary Islands is desalinated sea water. It is safe to drink, though doesn't taste particularly good and most locals buy bottled water, which is cheap and readily available. If you are in any doubt, ask *¿Es potable el agua (de grifo)?* – Is the (tap) water drinkable? Do not drink from lakes as they may contain bacteria or viruses that can cause diarrhoea or vomiting.

Biting the Package Bullet

Playa de las Américas is one of those rare hotel jungles where the high-profile tour operators often have amazing deals. Some of the most reputable agencies are Thomas Cook (www.thomascook.com), Tui (www.tui.co.uk), First Choice (www.firstchoice.co.uk) and Cosmos (www.cosmos.co.uk). If you decide to stake out your own accommodation and are planning on spending a few nights here, try apartment agencies first. A pleasant apartment for two, with a kitchen, a TV and a living area, starts at around €300 a week (generally the minimum booking period). Contact the tourist office for a full listing of agencies, or start with two firms in Los Cristianos that also have options in Playa de las Américas: **Anyka Sur** (Map p124, D7; 922 79 13 77; www.anykasur.com; Edificio Azahara, Avenida Habana, Los Cristianos; 9.30am-1.30pm & 5-8pm Mon-Fri) or **Marcus Management** (Map p124, E7; 922 75 10 64; www.tenerife-apts.com; Apartamentos Portosin, Avenida Penetración, Los Cristianos; 9am-5pm Mon-Fri, to 1pm Sat).

lessons, too. (922 75 05 13; https://k16surf.com; Paseo Orinoco, Playa de las Americas; 9am-10pm)

Artenerife
ARTS & CRAFTS

28 MAP P124, C4

Artenerife carries a superb range of quality handicrafts from the Canary Islands, including ceramics, jewellery and art. (www.artenerife.com; Avenida Rafael Puig Lluvina, Playa de las Américas; 10am-5pm Tue-Fri, to 1pm Sat, to 6pm Mon)

Bounty
FASHION & ACCESSORIES

29 MAP P124, C7

This exclusive boutique sells quality traditional and contemporary fashions for men and women. (922 28 82 11; Avenida Américas 56, Playa de las Américas; 10am-10pm Mon-Sat, 2-9pm Sun)

Joyería Pagodo
JEWELLERY

30 MAP P124, C7

An upmarket jewellery and watch shop with beautiful items, including from all the swanky, known brands like Versace, Mont Blanc, Gucci, Armani, Tissot and Swarovski. (922 79 11 05; www.grupopagoda.com; Avenida de las Américas 7, Playa de las Américas; 10am-10pm Mon-Sat)

Plaza del Duque
SHOPPING CENTRE

31 MAP P124, C1

This luxurious shopping centre has around 60 shops, including designer boutiques and a kids' zone, arranged within a circular building ringed by a roundabout. (www.plazadelduque.com; Playa del Duque, Costa Adeje; 10am-10pm;)

Worth a Trip 🥾
Parque Nacional del Teide

Standing sentry over Tenerife, formidable El Teide is the highest mountain in Spain and is the highlight of a trip to Tenerife. The surrounding national park, which covers 189.9 sq km and encompasses the volcano and the surrounding hinterland, is Spain's most popular national park. The area is truly extraordinary, comprising a haunting lunar moonscape of surreal rock formations, mystical caves and craggy peaks.

📞 922 01 04 40

www.volcanoteide.com

Carretera TF21

cable car adult/child €27/13.50

🕒 9am-5pm, to 7pm Jul-Sep, to 6pm Oct

Self-Guided Walks

The visitor guide lists 21 walks, varying in length from 600m to a strenuous 17.6km, some of which are signposted. Each walk is graded according to its level of difficulty. You are not allowed to stray from the marked trails, a sensible restriction in an environment where every tuft of plant life has to fight for survival.

Pico Viejo

A fabulous hike is to climb to the summit of Pico Viejo, then walk along the ridge that connects this mountain to Teide and on up to the summit. Allow nine hours (one way) and be prepared to walk back down Teide again if the cable car is closed. Consider staying overnight at the **Refugio de Altavista** (☑902 67 86 76; Cañadas del Teide; dm €21) at 3270m.

Climbing the Peak

Don't underestimate El Teide: it may not be the Himalaya, but it's still a serious undertaking. If you plan on climbing to the summit, you must reserve your place online at www.reservasparques-nacionales.es. You can reserve up to 2pm the day before you want to climb and choose from several two-hour slots per day in which to make your final ascent to the summit (however, permits are issued subject to availability). In addition to the permit, take along your passport or ID.

Roques de García

A few kilometres south of El Teide peak, across from the **Parador Nacional** (☑922 38 64 15; www.parador.es; d incl breakfast from €145; ❉✱✈✉), lies this extraordinary **geological formation** (pictured; TF-21; P) of twisted lava pinnacles with names like the Finger of God and the Cathedral. They are the result of the erosion of old volcanic dykes, or vertical

★ Top Tips

o Book your cable-car ticket online to reserve a slot.

o Avoid taking the cable car if you suffer from altitude sickness; walking and taking your time will help with acclimatisation.

✗ Take a Break

Parador Nacional, inside the park, has an excellent, elegant restaurant and a cafe with a terrace.

Alternatively, head to Vilaflor, where there's more eating choices, including **El Rincon de Roberto** (☑922 70 90 35; Avenida Hermano Pedro 27; mains €7.50-19; ◷noon-6pm Mon, to 10pm Wed-Sat, to 9pm Sun; ✱), which specialises in slow-cooked Canarian cuisine.

★ Getting There

Only two public buses service the park: bus 348 from Puerto de la Cruz (€6.20, one hour), and bus 342 from Los Cristianos (€7, 1½ hours).

streams of magma. A family-friendly 1½-hour trail leads around the Roques, where you won't need more than comfortable shoes and some warm clothing. Spreading out to the west are the otherworldly bald plains of the Llano de Ucanca. Parking here can be tricky when it's busy.

Cable Car to the Peak

The cable car provides the easiest, and most popular, way to reach the El Teide peak. On clear days, the volcanic peak spreads out majestically below and you can see the islands of La Gomera, La Palma and El Hierro peeking up from the Atlantic. It takes just eight minutes to zip up 1200m. Bring a warm jacket.

Observatorio del Teide

One of the best places in the northern hemisphere to stargaze is the Observatorio del Teide. Scientists come from the world over to study here. You can have a free tour, but you'll need to make an appointment first. For more information, check out www.iac.es. **Volcano Teide Experience** (📞922 01 04 44; www.volcanoteide.com; tour €30), a private tour company, runs daytime 90-minute tours (€21) to the observatory and also offers a number of eight-hour stargazing packages (starting from €50 per person).

Rocky landscape of Parque Nacional del Teide ROSSHELEN/GETTY IMAGES ©

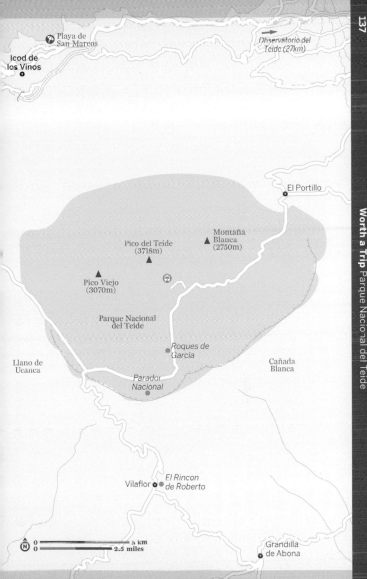

Icod de
los Vinos

Playa de
San Marcos

Observatorio del
Teide (27km)

El Portillo

Pico del Teide
(3718m)

Montaña
Blanca
(2750m)

Pico Viejo
(3070m)

Parque Nacional
del Teide

Roques de
Garcia

Llano de
Ucanca

Cañada
Blanca

Parador
Nacional

El Rincon
de Roberto

Vilaflor

Grandilla
de Abona

0   5 km
0   2.5 miles

Walking Tour 🥾

Village Life in Garachico

This gracious, tranquil town is located in a deep valley flanked by forested slopes and a rocky coastline. Sometimes bypassed by tourists, Garachico has managed to retain its intrinsic Canarian identity. Spend a few hours here, exploring the quaint cobbled streets, dipping into local tapas bars and absorbing the traditional culture and lifestyle.

Getting There

🚌 Bus 107 connects Garachico with Santa Cruz (€8.15, two hours), La Laguna, La Orotava and Icod de los Vinos. Bus 363 runs regularly from Puerto de la Cruz (€3.75, one hour).

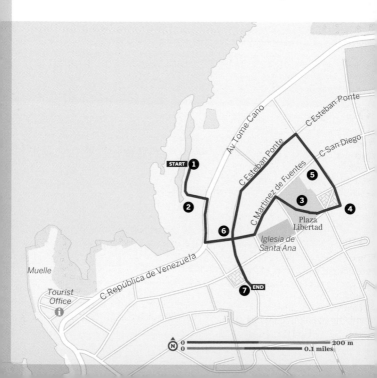

❶ Volcanic Coves

Strung along the seafront, these natural pools and channels known as **El Caletón** (Avenida Tomé Cano) were formed by the lava flow from a volcanic eruption in 1706, which buried half the town. Today they are ideal for paddling toddlers or swimming, some are even deep enough for diving.

❷ Waterfront Amble

Wander along the rocky-cove waterfront, past local fisherfolk waiting for a bite, and drop by the **Castillo de San Miguel** (Avenida Tomé Cano; adult/child €2/free; ⊙10am-4pm), which contains a modest two-room museum about the town's history, including exhibits on piracy, sea life and geology. Climb the tower for excellent views.

❸ Sitting in the Square

Stroll through one of Tenerife's most delightful plazas, **Plaza Libertad**, where old men in flat caps play cards or dominoes, surrounded by sauntering couples, children kicking balls and families shaded by Indian laurel trees. The kiosk-cafe here serves drinks and snacks.

❹ Pondering on the Past

On the corner of the plaza sits the gracious 16th-century **Convento de San Francisco** (Plaza Libertad; adult/child €2/free; ⊙11am-2pm & 3-6pm Mon-Fri, 10am-4pm Sat). This rambling museum here has exhibits set around beautiful cloisters, which include the volcanic history of the town and islands and some fascinating early-20th-century photos of the town.

❺ Tapas Time

Passing the sumptuous Hotel La Quinta Roja, head round the back to the delightful small bar **Tasca del Vino** (☎696 69 52 75; Glorieta de San Francisco; ⊙10am-10pm Mon-Sat), located on a picturesque cobbled side street beside the hotel. Here you can enjoy a drink with a generously portioned tapa for just €2.50.

❻ Potty About Pottery

Near here is a ceramic and art shop, which would look happily at home in any urban-chic big city. Run by German artist Alice Gauer and her Spanish partner Julian Betemps, **Art Shop** (www.artshop-garachico. com; Calle Esteban de Ponte 3; ⊙11am-8pm) has an eclectic display of art, including sea-urchin jewellery, carved wooden plates, paintings and contemporary ceramics.

❼ Puerta de Tierra (Land Gate)

A relic of the town's former life before it was redesigned by volcanic action, **Parque de la Puerta de Tierra** (Calle Juan González de la Torre) is a serene experience. The Puerta de Tierra (Land Gate) is all that's left of Garachico's once-thriving port. The gate once stood right on the water but thanks to the eruption it's now isolated in the centre of town.

Driving Tour 🛞

Exploring the Anaga Mountains

These stunning, rugged mountains are home to centuries' old laurel forests, tiny unspoiled villages and emerald-green valleys. They sprawl across the far northeast corner of the island and offer some of the most spectacular scenery in Tenerife. Unsurprisingly, this is one of the best regions for hiking on the island.

Getting There

🚌 There are frequent 910 buses (€1.25, 20 minutes) from Santa Cruz to San Andrés, which continue to Playa de las Teresitas– it's best to go by car from here.

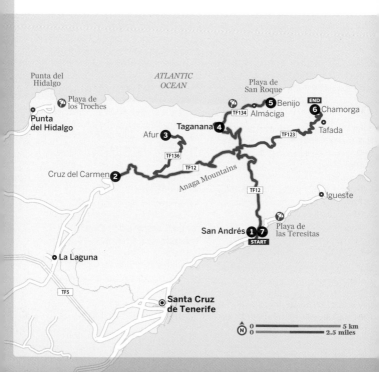

❶ Breakfast by the Beach

Head along the coast to **San Andrés**, with its narrow shady streets lined with fishers' cottages. Grab a coffee at **Bar El Peton** (14 Calle Aparejo; ⏱7am-7pm), then stroll to the end of the promenade to admire Playa de las Teresitas.

❷ Cruz del Carmen

The next destination is 29km away, but is an essential first stop for orienting yourself and understanding the wealth of regional hiking opportunities. The **Centro de Visitantes** (☎922 63 35 76; www.gaprural.com; Cruz del Carmen; ⏱9.30am-4pm) has an exhibition centre and information on 13 walks. There's also an excellent cafe, a chapel and ample parking, as well as a restaurant on the far side of the road.

❸ Picturesque Village

Take the TF-136 to **Afur**. This tranquil hamlet has just 15 residents and is located deep in a lush ravine, complete with bubbling stream. The village is just a dot on the map, with a bar, a shop and a sprinkling of houses set in the most delightful landscape. Several walks are signposted from the car park here.

❹ The Oldest Town

Back on the TF-12, follow the signs to Taganana on the TF-134; this steep winding road, which eventually leads to the coast, is one of the most stunning in the mountain range. Dating from the 16th century.

Taganana is the largest and oldest town in the region. Explore the atmospheric cobbled streets and the Iglesia de Las Nieves.

❺ Seafood & Cheese

Carry on to the blink-and-you-miss-it hamlet of **Benijo** (population around 20) overlooking the sea, and stop off at the seafood restaurant, **El Fronton** (☎922 59 02 38; Pista al Draguillo 1; mains €7-9; ⏱10am-7.30pm); try the simple grilled fresh fish with *mojo* (Canarian spicy sauce) potatoes. Afterwards stroll 250m up the hill to Casa Paca, a local producer of goat's cheese.

❻ Isolated Hamlet

Continue past El Draguillo where the road heads inland to **Chamorga**, another tiny hamlet nestled in a verdant palm-studded valley. Have a coffee at **Bar Casa Álvaro** (Carretera Chamorga 21; ⏱11am-5pm) and explore the streets lined with traditional houses featuring hipped Moorish-style tile roofs.

❼ Fish Dinner

Return to San Andrés via the TF-123 and the TF-12. End your day with a seafood dinner at the **Cofradía de Pescadores** (☎922 54 90 24; www.lacofradiadepescadores.es; Avenida Marítimo de San Andrés; mains €10-18; ⏱11am-11pm Wed-Sat, to 10pm Sun, to 4pm Mon), which is owned by the local fishers, so your seafood really will be as fresh as that day's catch.

Survival Guide

Before You Go

Book Your Stay

○ Outside Carnaval time, finding a room is generally not a problem in Santa Cruz and the north of the island.

○ Book in advance when possible for the south, particularly around Los Cristianos and Playa de las Américas.

Useful Websites

Casas Rurales (www. ecoturismocanarias. com) An extensive selection of rural accommodation across the island.

Lonely Planet (www. lonelyplanet.com/can ary-islands/tenerife/ hotels) Recommenda- tions and bookings.

Tenerife Holiday Apartments (www.tha- tenerife.co.uk) Over 150 apartments and villas for holiday rental.

Country Houses (www.ruraltenerife. net) Rural cottages and traditional Canarian country houses for rent.

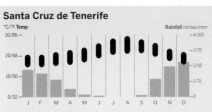

Santa Cruz de Tenerife

When to Go

○ **Winter (Dec–Feb)** Pleasantly warm, ex- cept on El Teide, where deep winter can result in snowfall closing the mountain.

○ **Spring (Mar–Apr)** Good for hiking and seeing wildflowers. Surfers are rewarded with the best waves in March.

○ **Summer (May– Sep)** Expect around 11 hours of daily sunshine. The average is 28°C in August.

○ **Autumn (Oct–Nov)** Temperatures fall to around 21°C. There are fewer tourists, and some hotels may drop their prices slightly.

Best Budget

El Jostel (www. eljostel.com) Adorable four-room hostel in Santa Cruz.

Albergue Montes de Anaga (www. alberguestenerife.net) A pocket-friendly hiker's hostel in the mountains.

Bed & Breakfast La Laguna (www.bbla laguna.com) A cross between a B&B and a hostel, with a commu- nity kitchen and shared bathrooms.

Hotel Adonis Capital (www.adonisresorts. com) Centrally located option offering excellent value in Santa Cruz.

Pension Cejas (www. pensioncejas.com) Long-running pension with bright, colourful rooms and a friendly welcome.

Best Midrange

Hotel Alhambra (www. alhambra-orotava.com) Gorgeous art-filled manor house in La Orotava.

Hotel La Quinta Roja
(www.quintaroja.com)
Serene rooms in a
restored 16th-century
manor house in the
centre of Garachico.

Hotel Victoria (www.
hotelruralvictoria.com)
Boutique hotel in an
exquisite 17th-century
mansion in La Orotava.

Hotel Tigaiga (www.
tigaiga.com) Bright and
colourful rooms set in
beautiful gardens in
Puerto de la Cruz.

La Laguna Gran Hotel
(www.lalagunagra
nhotel.com) As well
as elegant rooms, this
hotel boasts an excel-
lent Michelin-starred
restaurant.

Best Top End

**Iberostar Grand
Mencey** (www.iberos-
tar.com) Elegant five-
star option set in lovely
gardens in the capital.

**Hard Rock Hotel Ten-
erife** (www.hardrock
hotels.com) An excel-
lent family-friendly
resort in Costa Adeje.

Baobab Suites (www.
baobabsuites.com)
These elegant suites
in Costa Adeje boast
private pools and ocean
views.

Parador Nacional
(www.paradores.es)
Attractive hotel in
the heart of Parque
Nacional del Teide.

Europe Villa Cortés
(www.europe-hotels.
org) Truly sumptuous
hotel designed in the
style of an ultraluxuri-
ous Mexican hacienda.

Arriving in Tenerife

Tenerife Sur Airport

About 20km east of
Playa de las Américas,
Tenerife Sur (☎922 75
95 10; www.aena.es; Reina
Sofía) is the main inter-
national airport.

Tenerife Norte Airport

Located near Santa
Cruz in the north of
the island, **Tenerife
Norte** (☎902 40 47 04,
922 63 56 35; www.aena.
es; Los Rodeos) mostly
handles interisland
flights.

Estación Marítima Muelle Ribera

Buy tickets for all ferry
companies with routes
to and from Tenerife
from travel agents
or from the main
**Estación Marítima
Muelle Ribera** (Map
p44) in Santa Cruz de
Tenerife.

Trasmediterránea (Map
p44; ☎In Madrid 902 45 46
45; www.trasmediterranea.
com; 39 Calle la Marina)
runs a ferry at 11.59pm
every Friday from
Santa Cruz that makes
the following stops:

○ Las Palmas de Gran
Canaria, Gran Canaria
(from €27, 8½ hours)

○ Puerto del Rosario,
Fuerteventura (from
€32, 20½ hours)

○ Arrecife, Lanzarote
(from €35, 24 hours)

Naviera Armas (Map
p44; ☎902 45 65 00; www.
navieraarmas.com) runs an
extensive ferry service
around the islands
from Santa Cruz, to the
following locations:

○ Las Palmas de Gran
Canaria, Gran Canaria
(from €38, 2½ hours, 21
weekly)

○ Morro Jable,
Fuerteventura (from €70,
6½ hours, one daily)

○ Puerto del Rosario, Fuerteventura (from €83, 11½ hours, one daily)

○ Arrecife, Lanzarote (from €94, 11 hours, one daily Monday to Friday)

Fred Olsen (Map p44; ☏ 902 10 01 07; www. fredolsen.es; ⊙ telephone enquiries 8am-8pm) has three to six daily ferries from Santa Cruz to Agaete in the northwest of Gran Canaria (€42, 1¼ hours), from where you can take its free bus onwards to Las Palmas (35 minutes).

Los Cristianos Ferry Terminal

Ferries run in and out of the Los Cristianos port day and night. **Naviera Armas** (p145) and the faster but more expensive **Fred Olsen** services operate from here. Tickets are available from travel agents or from the main Estación Marítima building.

Routes operated by Naviera Armas from Los Cristianos include the following:

○ San Sebastián de la Gomera, La Gomera (€32, one hour, three daily Monday to Friday, one Saturday, two Sunday)

○ Santa Cruz de la Palma, La Palma (€46, 3½ hours, one daily Sunday to Friday)

○ Valverde, El Hierro (€50, 3¾ hours, daily Sunday to Friday)

Routes operated by Fred Olsen from Los Cristianos include the following:

○ San Sebastián de la Gomera, La Gomera (€34, 50 minutes, three daily Monday to Friday, two daily Saturday and Sunday)

○ Santa Cruz de la Palma, La Palma (from €48, two hours, one daily Sunday to Friday)

Getting Around

Bus

○ **TITSA** (Transportes Interurbanos de Tenerife SA; ☏ 922 53 13 00; www.titsa. com; ⊙ customer service 8am-8pm) runs bus services all over the island, as well as within Santa Cruz and other towns.

○ If you'll be travelling a lot by public transport then it is worth investing in a plastic Ten+ Travel Card.

○ The card can be used on all bus routes (except on Teide and Teno lines) and offers 30% off the trip fare.

○ The travel card costs €2, with top-ups from a minimum of €5 to a maximum of €100.

○ Swipe your card when you board and swipe off as you disembark.

○ The same card can be used by several users.

○ Bus line 343 (€9.70) links Tenerife Norte Airport with Tenerife Sur Airport.

Car

○ Renting a car in Tenerife is highly recommended; the bus service is good but restricts you timewise and exploring inland is only really possible with your own wheels.

○ All the major international car-rental companies are represented in Tenerife and there are also plenty of local operators.

- To rent a car you need to have a driving licence, be aged 21 or over, and, for the major companies at least, have a credit card.

- Rent your car online before you travel, to both save money and also avoid being in a situation where there are no available cars for rental (it can happen in high season).

- Third-party motor insurance is a minimum requirement when renting a car in Tenerife.

- Generally, you're not supposed to take a hire car from one island to another without the company's explicit permission

- Speed limits in built-up areas: 50km/h, which increases to 100km/h on major roads and up to 120km/h on *autovías* (highways).

Taxi

- You can take a taxi anywhere on the island – but it is an expensive way to get around.

Tram

- A tram line (www.metrotenerife.com) links

Dos & Don'ts

Greetings Spaniards almost always greet friends and strangers alike with a kiss on each cheek, although two males only do this if they're close friends.

Church visits It is considered rather disrespectful to visit churches for the purposes of tourism during Mass and other worship services.

Punctuality As with mainland Spain, timeliness is not held in such high regard as it may be in other European nations, so try to go with the flow.

central Santa Cruz with La Laguna.

- Tickets cost €1.35 and the full journey takes 40 minutes.

Essential Information

Business Hours

The following standard opening hours are for high season only:

Banks 8.30am–2pm Monday to Friday

Bars 7pm–midnight

Post offices 8.30am–8.30pm Monday to Friday, 9.30am–1pm Saturday (large cities): 8.30am–2.30pm Monday to Friday,

9.30am–1pm Saturday (elsewhere)

Restaurants Meals served 1pm–4pm and 7pm–late

Shops 10am–2pm and 5pm–9pm Monday to Friday, 10am–2pm Saturday

Supermarkets 9am–9pm Monday to Saturday

Discount Cards

To receive any available discounts, photo ID is essential.

- Seniors get reduced prices at various museums and attractions and occasionally on transport. The minimum age varies between 60 and 65 years.

o Students receive discounts of usually half the normal fee, though student cards are not accepted everywhere.

o Ask at individual tourist offices for discount cards covering local attractions.

Electricity

**Type C
230V/50Hz**

LGBT+ Travellers

o Gay and lesbian marriages are both legal in Spain and hence on the Canary Islands.

o Spanish people generally adopt a live-and-let-live attitude to sexuality, so you shouldn't have any hassles in Tenerife.

o Some small rural towns may not quite know how

to deal with overt displays of affection between same-sex couples.

Money
ATMs

o Multilingual *cajeros automáticos* (ATMs) are widely available

o There's usually a charge of between 2% and 3% on ATM cash withdrawals abroad.

Credit cards

All major *tarjetas de crédito* (credit cards) and debit cards are widely accepted and can be used for many purchases including at petrol stations and larger supermarkets, which sometimes ask to see some form of ID.

Smaller establishments tend to accept cash only.

Money Changers

o Exchange facilities can be found at most air and sea ports.

o Usually indicated by the word *cambio* (exchange).

o Usually offer longer opening hours and quicker service than banks, and in many cases, better rates.

Tipping

o Not obligatory but most people at least leave small change.

o Five percent is normally fine and 10% considered generous.

o Porters will generally be happy with €1.

o Round up to the nearest euro in taxis.

Public Holidays

Many shops are closed and many attractions operate with reduced hours on the following dates:

Año Nuevo (New Year's Day) 1 January

Día de los Reyes Magos (Three Kings Day) 6 January

Viernes Santo (Good Friday) March/April

Fiesta del Trabajo (Labour Day) 1 May

La Asunción de la Virgen (Feast of the Assumption) 15 August

Día de la Hispanidad (National Day) 12 October

Todos los Santos (All Saints' Day) 1 November

La Inmaculada Concepción (Feast of the Immaculate Conception) 8 December

Navidad (Christmas)
25 December

In addition, the regional government sets a further five holidays, while local councils allocate another two. Common holidays include the following:

Martes de Carnival (Carnival Tuesday) February/March

Día de San Juan (St John's Day) 19 March

Jueves Santo (Maundy Thursday) March/April

Día de las Islas Canarias (Canary Islands Day) 30 May

Corpus Christi (the Thursday after the eighth Sunday after Easter Sunday) June

Día de Santiago Apóstol (Feast of St James the Apostle, Spain's patron saint) 25 July; in Santa Cruz de Tenerife the day also marks the commemoration of the defence of the city against British Admiral Nelson.

Día de la Constitución (Constitution Day) 6 December

Safe Travel

In terms of personal security, Tenerife generally feels safe and nonthreatening. The main thing to be wary of is petty theft.

o Keep valuables concealed or locked in your hotel room and don't leave anything on display in your car.

o Be wary of pickpockets in areas with plenty of other tourists.

o Women travellers may encounter sexual harassment; this is often nothing more sinister than catcalling or staring, but it is enough to be intimidating.

o Watch out for rip tides when swimming on all the islands.

Telephone Services

o Buy a pay-as-you-go mobile with credit from €30. Local SIM cards are widely available and can be used in unlocked GSM phones. If you have a GSM, dual- or tri-band cellular mobile phone you can buy SIM cards and prepaid time.

o All the Spanish phone companies (including Orange, Vodafone and Movistar) offer prepaid accounts for mobiles. You can then top up the cards in their shops or outlets, such as supermarkets and tobacconists.

o The Canaries uses GSM 900/1800, which is compatible with the rest of Europe and Australia but not with the North American GSM 1900 or the system used in Japan.

o From those countries, you will need to travel with a tri-band or quadric-band phone.

o Mobile numbers start with a 6.

Phone Codes

International access code	☎ 00
Country code	☎ 34
National toll-free number	☎ 900

Money-Saving Tips

o For inexpensive restaurant dining order the *menú del día* (set menu) for lunch.

o Look out for free entry to sights, often on the first Sunday of the month.

Island area codes

∘ Gran Canaria, Lanzarote, Fuerteventura
☏928

∘ Tenerife, La Gomera, La Palma and El Hierro
☏922

Toilets

Public toilets are not common and not always too pleasant. The easiest option is to wander into a bar or cafe and use its facilities. The polite thing to do is to make a small purchase, but you're unlikely to raise too many eyebrows if you don't.

The cautious carry some toilet paper with them when out and about as many toilets don't have it. If there's a bin beside the toilet, put paper and so on in it – probably because the local sewage system has trouble coping.

Tourist Information

∘ All major towns have a tourist office where you will usually get decent maps and information about sights and activities.

∘ The major airports also have tourist offices and can usually assist with last-minute accommodation bookings.

Visas

Citizens/residents of EU and Schengen countries No visa required.

Citizens/residents of Australia, Canada, Israel, Japan, NZ and USA No visa required for tourist visits of up to 90 days.

Anaga Mountains (p140)

Language

Spanish (español) – often referred to as castellano (Castilian) to distinguish it from other languages spoken in Spain – is the language of Tenerife. While you'll find an increasing number of locals who speak some English, don't count on it. Travellers who learn a little Spanish will be amply rewarded as Spaniards appreciate the effort, no matter how basic your understanding of the language.

Most Spanish sounds are pronounced the same as their English counterparts. Those familiar with Spanish might notice the Andalusian or even Latin American lilt of the Canarian accent – 'lli' is pronounced as y and the 'lisp' you might expect with 'z' and 'c' before vowels sounds more like s while the letter 's' itself is hardly pronounced at all. If you follow our pronunciation guides (with the stressed syllables in italics) you'll be understood just fine. Note that 'm/f' indicates masculine and feminine forms.

To enhance your trip with a phrasebook, visit **lonelyplanet. com**.

Basics

Hello.
Hola.   o·la

Goodbye.
Adiós.   a·dyos

How are you?
¿Qué tal?   ke tal

Fine, thanks.
Bien, gracias.   byen gra·syas

Please.
Por favor.   por fa·vor

Thank you.
Gracias.   gra·syas

Excuse me.
Perdón.   per·don

Sorry.
Lo siento.   lo syen·to

Yes./No.
Sí./No.   see/no

Do you speak (English)?
¿Habla (inglés)?   a·bla (een·gles)

I (don't) understand.
Yo (no) entiendo.   yo (no) en·tyen·do

What's your name?
¿Cómo se   ko·mo se
llama?   lya·ma

My name is ...
Me llamo ...   me lya·mo ...

Eating & Drinking

What would you recommend?
¿Qué   ke
recomienda?   re·ko·myen·da

Cheers!
¡Salud!   sa·loo

That was delicious!
¡Estaba   es·ta·ba
buenísimo!   bwe·nee·see·mo

The bill, please.
La cuenta,   la kwen·ta
por favor.   por ta·vor

I'd like ...
Quisiera ...   kee·sye·ra ...

a coffee	un café	oon ka·fe
a table for two	una mesa para dos	oo·na me·sa pa·ra dos
two beers	dos cervezas	dos ser·ve·sas

Shopping

I'd like to buy ...
Quisiera comprar ... — kee·sye·ra kom·prar ...

Can I look at it?
¿Puedo verlo? — pwe·do ver·lo

How much is it?
¿Cuánto cuesta? — kwan·to kwes·ta

Can you lower the price?
¿Podría bajar un poco el precio? — po·dree·a ba·khar oon po·ko el pre·syo

Emergencies

Help!
¡Socorro! — so·ko·ro

Call a doctor!
¡Llame a un médico! — lya·me a oon me·dee·ko

Call the police!
¡Llame a la policía! — lya·me a la po·lee·see·a

I'm lost. (m/f)
Estoy perdido/a. — es·toy per·dee·do/a

I'm ill. (m/f)
Estoy enfermo/a. — es·toy en·fer·mo/a

Time & Numbers

What time is it?
¿Qué hora es? — ke o·ra es

It's (10) o'clock.
Son (las diez). — son (las dyes)

morning	mañana	ma·nya·na
afternoon	tarde	tar·de
evening	noche	no·che
yesterday	ayer	a·yer
today	hoy	oy
tomorrow	mañana	ma·nya·na

1	uno	oo·no
2	dos	dos
3	tres	tres
4	cuatro	kwa·tro
5	cinco	seen·ko
6	seis	seys
7	siete	sye·te
8	ocho	o·cho
9	nueve	nwe·ve
10	diez	dyes

Transport & Directions

Where's ...?
¿Dónde está ...? — don·de es·ta ...

Where's the station?
¿Dónde está la estación? — don·de es·ta la es·ta·syon

What's the address?
¿Cuál es la dirección? — kwal es la dee·rek·syon

Can you show me (on the map)?
¿Me lo puede indicar (en el mapa)? — me lo pwe·de een·dee·kar (en el ma·pa)

I want to go to ...
Quisiera ir a ... — kee·sye·ra eer a ...

What time does it arrive/leave?
¿A qué hora llega/sale? — a ke o·ra lye·ga/sa·le

I want to get off here.
Quiero bajarme aquí. — kye·ro ba·khar·me a·kee

Behind the Scenes

Send Us Your Feedback

We love to hear from travellers – your comments help make our books better. We read every word, and we guarantee that your feedback goes straight to the authors. Visit **lonelyplanet.com/contact** to submit your updates and suggestions.

Note: We may edit, reproduce and incorporate your comments in Lonely Planet products such as guidebooks, websites and digital products, so let us know if you don't want your comments reproduced or your name acknowledged. For a copy of our privacy policy visit lonelyplanet.com/privacy.

Lucy's Thanks

Many thanks to Jessica Ryan and the LP team for the cheery support and to Damian Harper for bringing his passion for Tenerife to the pages of this guide.

Damian's Thanks

Many thanks to Isabella Noble for all her support and good humour, gratitude to the ever-helpful Li Jiani and Arman, cheers also to Juan de la Vega, Damien, Carlos Brito, Olga Aresté, Ellen, Ling, Michele, Tim and Emma, and everyone else along the way who made this trip such a fascinating journey of discovery.

Acknowledgements

Cover photograph: Las Teresitas with scenic San Andrés village, leoks/Shutterstock ©

This Book

This 2nd edition of Lonely Planet's *Pocket Tenerife* guidebook was researched and written by Damian Harper, and curated by Lucy Corne. The previous edition was written by Josephine Quintero. This guidebook was produced by the following:

Destination Editor Tom Stainer

Senior Product Editors Jessica Ryan, Genna Patterson

Regional Senior Cartographer Anthony Phelan

Product Editors Kate McNamara, Ronan Abayawickrema, Amy Lynch, Claire Rourke

Book Designer Jessica Rose

Assisting Editors Nigel Chin, Gabrielle Innes, Lou McGregor, Charlotte Orr

Assisting Cartographers Hunor Csutoros, Julie Dodkins

Cover Researcher Naomi Parker

Thanks to Gwen Cotter, Dr Andy Drummond, Sandie Kestell, Catherine Naghten, Amanda Williamson

Index

See also separate subindexes for:
Eating p156
Drinking p157
Entertainment p157
Shopping p158

Sights 000
Map Pages **000**

🔒 Shopping

LONELY PLANET IN THE WILD

Our Writers

Lucy Corne

Lucy left university with a degree in journalism and a pair of perpetually itchy feet. She taught EFL for eight years in Spain, South Korea, Canada, China and India, while writing freelance features for a range of magazines, newspapers and websites. She joined the Lonely Planet team in 2008 and has since worked on a range of titles including *Africa, Canary Islands* and *South Africa, Lesotho & Swaziland,* and several other titles. Lucy lives in Cape Town with her husband and young son, where she writes on travel, food and beer. Her popular blog, www.brewmistress.co.za, documents the South African beer scene.

Damian Harper

Born off the Strand within earshot of Bow Bells (favourable wind permitting), Damian grew up in Notting Hill way before it was discovered by Hollywood. A onetime Shakespeare and Company bookseller and radio presenter, Damian has been writing guidebooks for Lonely Planet since the late 1990s. He lives in South London with his wife and two kids, and frequently returns to China (his second home).

Published by Lonely Planet Global Limited
CRN 554153
2nd edition – Jan 2020
ISBN 9781786575838
© Lonely Planet 2020 Photographs © as indicated 2020
10 9 8 7 6 5 4 3 2 1
Printed in Malaysia